IKEBANA
WITH THE SEASONS

IKEBANA WITH THE SEASONS

KOZAN OKADA

SHUFUNOTOMO CO., LTD.

Third printing, 1992

Photography: Kenji Ugaki
Book Design: Momoyo Nishimura
Editors: Mutsumi Horikoshi
Michiko Kinoshita
English Text: Hollistar Ferretti

Published by SHUFUNOTOMO CO., LTD.
2-9, Kanda Surugadai, Chiyoda-ku, Tokyo,
101 Japan

ISBN: 4-07-975345-4
Printed in Japan

PREFACE

In the last few years, I have ventured into the unexplored world of "the flowers of the field." In my encounter with over a thousand species of wild flowers, through ikebana I have been able to express my feelings toward the universe, both heaven and earth.

I would like to share my experiences with you by presenting them in the order of the four seasons. The first theme is "Ikebana with the Seasons" and the second, "Wild Flowers and Creative Work."

In "Ikebana with the Seasons," I used cultivated flowers, such as you buy from the florist or grow in your garden. I paid special attention to imparting a sense of the seasons as I tried to seek out new expressions to match our contemporary lifestyle.

For example, when arranging just a few flowers in a large container, I tried to give importance to the character of the floral material so it was not overshadowed by the container. If the branches of the material had few redeeming qualities, I sought beauty in the leaves and flowers.

In "Wild Flowers and Creative Work," I tried to express in a simple and straightforward manner, the rich poetic beauty of wild plants in their natural setting in accordance to the four seasons. It is a manifestation of my admiration of the power, beauty and greatness of Mother Nature.

I roamed through the fields and hills of Bonari Heights in Inawashiro-cho, Fukushima Prefecture. Inspired by the natural beauty I found, I immersed myself in creating ikebana through spring, summer and fall, giving myself body and soul to the natural splendor I discovered.

Each arrangement I have introduced here reflects the wonder I feel towards the plant world. I have felt the miracle of trees sprouting buds in the spring, the fulfilled promise of flowers in bloom, the beauty of the delicately different shades of fresh green leaves, the playfulness of vines swaying in a summer breeze, the pageantry of brightly colored flowers of summer, the inviting coolness of shade trees, the glory of fields ablaze with autumn flowers, and the grandeur of leaves turning color. The ephemeral quality of all plant life, makes it all the more precious.

I would like to express my gratitude to Mr. Hajime Onodera of the Man'yo Garden. Through his kind cooperation, I had the opportunity of making the acquaintance of many rare alpine plants. Thanks to his encouragement, I could arrange more than three hundred different materials.

I am also indebted to the good offices of Shufunotomo Co., Ltd., International Department for this English language edition.

Kozan Okada

Kozan Okada

The History of the Kozan School

The Kozan School, established toward the end of the Meiji Period represented a new ikebana concept, a discipline emphasizing the natural characteristics of plants.

Kozan Okada I, born in 1876 in Hamamatsu, was apprenticed to the Ikenobo School of Ikebana by the time he was fifteen. The gifted young man applied himself diligently. As pupil of Shoan Mutoh, he went on to study under Sensei and Senkei, succeeding generations of Ikenobo iemoto. Devoting himself to the mastery of ikebana, he advanced in the Ikenobo hierarchy to earn their highest official title.

Recognized and respected as an ikebana artist, Kozan Okada I had the honor of arranging the solemn, ceremonial *rikka* and *seika* at the thrones of Their Imperial Majesties the Emperor and Empress of Meiji, Taisho and the present Showa. He was also privileged to arrange these traditional forms of ikebana for other members of the Imperial family, for visiting heads of state and other foreign officials in Japan and as floral tributes for state functions such as ship launchings. Drafts of the designs for those arrangements remain in the archives to this day.

Kozan Okada I was fascinated with the growing processes of iris during the four seasons. Making a study of this life cycle, he explored a new path of ikebana, one that opened up the possibilities of giving prominence to the natural beauty of plants, forms of Mother Nature which transcend human intelligence. He devised *nageire* and *moribana* arrangements in *jiyuuka*, free form. Using a variety of material and containers, his *jiyuuka* suited the architectural style of the time.

Kozan officially introduced his *jiyuuka nageire* for the first time to the throne of the Emperor in 1910, the 43rd year of Meiji. Because of this, this new style of arrangement is considered to have been established at that date.

Kozan's *jiyuuka* did not fit with the staid traditions of the Ikenobo School of that time. To give this contemporary ikebana statement room to grow, the Kozan School was established.

A course of instructions for Kozan's *jiyuuka* appeared serially in several women's magazines. It was also introduced throughout Japan in 1926, the 15th year of Taisho, via another media, an NHK radio program, for the first time.

To commemorate the Meiji Centennial in 1968, Kozan Okada I bestowed the title of Iemoto on Juko Nishimura, who became Kozan Okada II. Later that same year, the current Iemoto succeeded as Kozan Okada III.

Kozan Okada III studied under the demanding guidance of her grandfather Kozan Okada I from the time she was very young. As Iemoto, she continues to adapt ikebana to today's lifestyle, much as her grandfather did at the turn of the century. *Jiyuuka* in *nageire*, *moribana*, *morimono* and *shohin-bana* are carried on in the spirit of Kozan Okada I. She strives to popularize the ikebana of Kozan School, bringing it to the attention of the public and teaching the principles to her students. In 1974, she published her first book, "Four Seasons of Kozan Flower Arrangements."

Kozan Okada's activities as the third Iemoto include teaching, demonstrating and exhibiting at home and abroad. Examples of ikebana in daily life are introduced in the five books she written on the subject, including "The Flowers in the Fields and Mountains." In her study of wild plant life, she has arranged close to nine hundred kinds of wild plants and trees, giving insight to the beauty she finds in each.

The Kozan School heightens the awareness of the natural beauty within reach, opening our eyes to the wonder of nature. Kozan Okada III is as innovative as her predecessor, the renowned Kozan Okada I.

CONTENTS

PART I

IKEBANA WITH THE SEASONS

Material: Lichen covered pine, Japanese quince and chrysanthemum
Container: Kiseto vase

Kiseto is glazed ceramic ware prized for its distinctive yellow color caused by the oxidation of celadon glazes, and also for its beautiful dark iron-brown glaze. Chrysanthemums suit this type of a vase better than Western flowers. The lichen covered pine reenforces the mood while the branch of Japanese quince adds a bright note.

Material: Pine and rose
Container: Earthenware vessel

The combination of pine and rose signifies perpetual youth and eternal spring. The evergreen pine is said to stay green for a thousand years, and the rose suggests the promise of spring. This combination is appropriate for the celebration of the New Year.

Be sure to remove every withered pine needle and do not forget to cut the stems of the roses in water (*mizukiri*) before arranging them in the vase.

Material: *Daio-matsu* longleaf pine, red-budded willow, spirea thunbergii, tulip and baby's breath
Container: Low basin

I have arranged the manly *daio-matsu* along with sweeping branches of sprouting red-budded willow for asymmetrical contrast. I then placed spirea thunbergii with its gentle white blossoms in the middle and added red tulips to firm up the base.

Material: Japanese quince, Japanese red pine and narcissus
Container: Celadon basin

Japanese quince seems to branch out haphazardly and can be difficult to handle at times, but it can impart a carefree, yet elegant air if you arrange just a few. Train the pine along the base. When arranging narcissus in winter, arrange the flowers lower than leaves, trying not to impair the purity of the narcissus.

Text on page 130.

Material: Japanese quince and a budding camellia branch
Container: Wide-mouthed *Sue* vase by Moritoshi Tokuzawa

I tried to maintain the natural sprightly line and the buoyancy of Japanese quince. The camellia branch, with only one white bud partially opened, added a charming touch.

Material: Spike winter hazel (*Corylopsis spicata* Sieb. et Zucc.) and camellia
Container: Nanban pot

I angled a branch of spike winter hazel to reach out from a symmetrical, sober container. Considering the line, I trimmed away all unnecessary sprigs. I then arranged the camellias in a low position for balance and to firm up the base, paying attention to each and every leaf in the arrangement.

Material: Lily magnolia, reeves spirea and weeping forsythia
Container: Contemporary vase

Flowering trees look so beautiful in the springtime. Lily magnolias blooming on an elegant old tree under a spring sky always tempt me. I yearn to arrange them.

Magnolias are generous, beautiful flowers. It is important to stress characteristics in the arrangement.

Material: Peach blossom and rape blossom
Container: Rectangular basin

Try not to impair the simple beauty of the peach blossoms and stress the vigor of the young shoots as they healthily thrust out from the mother branch. The rape blossoms should be cut short and placed low in the arrangement.

Material: *Unryu* weeping willow and *akebono* camellia
Container: Koguryo celadon vase

The crooked branches of the *unryu* weeping willow create a light rhythmic pattern as they interwine with each other.
The light pink *akebono* camellias look gentle and graceful, giving quite a different impression than the sturdy, handsome wild camellia.
The Koguryo celadon vase has a cold dignity, but the amusing presentation of the *unryu* weeping willow, just beginning to put forth buds, and the *akebono* camellia softens the overall atmosphere.

Material: Spirea thunbergii and tulip
Container: Glass vase

With this cobalt blue glassware, I used only white flowers. One long branch of spirea thunbergii was arranged to the left side and several shorter lengths were massed at the base of the arrangement. The three tulips stand straight to create a simple visual impression.

Material: Cape marigold (*Dimorphotheca sinuata* DC.)
Container: Glass vase

I used only dimorphotheca with its spiked petaled orange flowers and supple stalks in this pure white container. Considering the uniqueness of the stalks and the size of the flowers, I arranged them freely in the tall vase.

Material: Freesia, pansy and asparagus
Container: Glass basin

Two kinds of spring flowers and the gracefully flowing soft green fern arranged in pastel glassware are an expression of spring. Since the asparagus has very fine stems, I fastened a few pieces together with rubber bands.

Material: Reeves spirea and Iceland poppy
Container: Round basin

One branch of the reeves spirea soars high over an arrangement of shorter branches. The addition of poppies with their curving stalks and colorful flowers suggests the arrival of spring. ▶

Material: *Miyako*-hill cherry, *unryu* weeping willow and Solomon's seal (*Polygonatum odoratum* Druce)
Container: Ceramic basin

The *Miyako*-hill cherry is considered the newest type of cherry blossom. This piece represents the tranquility of promise fulfilled with the gorgeous cherry blossoms predominating. The budded willow and the variegated green of the Solomon's seal form the base.

When arranging cherry blossoms, the blossoms take precedence over the line of the branches. Concentrate on exploiting the beauty of the blossoms.

Material: Japanese hill cherry (*Prunus jamasakura* Sieb.), *higanzakura* (*Prunus subhirtella* Miq.), *Yoshino* cherry (*Prunus yedoensis* Matsumura), double cherry blossom (*Prunus lannesiala* Wilson) and Japanese maple
Container: Large earthen pot

The light pink blossoms of the wild cherry found in the mountains in early spring and the dark pink double cherry blossoms of the villages in late spring are combined in a great pot to create a gorgeous atmosphere. The Japanese maple adds the fresh green color of spring foliage.

Material: Alpine azalea (*Rhododendron obtusum* Series)
Container: Nanban vase with ears

Alpine azalea is considered difficult material to arrange by itself. The important thing is to not impair the natural shape of the branches, both those which reach out and those used to firm up the base. In this arrangement, I wanted to stress the hardiness of the flower which blooms high in the mountains, weathering wind and snow.

◀ Material: Wisteria, azalea and rabbit-ear iris (*Iris laevigata* Fischer)
Container: Shigaraki pot by Hosei Okano

This arrangement combines three elegant flowers mentioned in Man'yo-shu, the earliest extant anthology of Japanese poetry from the fourth to the eighth centuries. The combination of the textured Shigaraki pot and the green of the iris leaves unwittingly created a calm, subdued atmosphere.

As wisteria does not easily absorb water, it is necessary to pour alcohol over it when cutting the branch from the vine and to immediately put it into water. Shave off the bark at the cut end of the branch, split the end and then dip it again in alcohol before arranging it in the vase.

Material: Double cherry blossom and fullmoon maple
Container: A deep Kiseto bowl

The double cherry blooms a bit later than the wild cherry. It is fascinating to see the exuberance of the blossoms. I tried to place full focus on the luxuriant blossoms in this Kiseto container and added but a single branch of fullmoon maple to further emphasize the resplendent flowering material.

Material: Japanese maple, China aster and Solomon's seal (*Polygonatum odoratum* Druce)
Container: Footed white porcelain basin

The fresh new green leaves beginning to unfurl on an old Japanese maple tree proclaim the miracle of spring. The shape of the gnarled branch with it's delicate leaves presents a striking picture against the *shoji* (sliding paper door).

The purple China aster is a pretty flower that looks gracefully modest in the white porcelain basin. The refreshing green and white Solomon's seal gives balance and successfully firms up the arrangement.

Material: *Omurasaki* azalea (*Rhododendron pulchrum* Sweet) and Solomon's seal (*Polygonatum odoratum* Druce)
Container: Bizen vase

Azaleas normally bear luxuriant blossoms, covering the branches like burning flames. For this Bizen vase, however, I picked supple branches of this species of azalea to produce a light appearance. Azalea branches often grow sideways and cannot be shaped for ikebana. It is necessary to trim the branches without losing the natural form.

Material: Yulan (*Magnolia denudata Desr.*) and red-veined maple
Container: Modified vase

Yulan, the magnolia tree native to China, puts forth large, pure white flowers before leaves appear. It is one of the cleanest and most beautiful of the spring flowers and trees. I decided to add the fresh new leaves of the red veined maple to add dimension to the mature magnolia branches, pointing up the beauty of the flowers. It turned out to be a refreshing combination.

Text on page 130.

Text on page 130.

Material: Japanese cucumber tree (*Magnolia obovata* Thunb.), mountain ash (*Sorbus commixta* Hedl.), arrowwood (*Viburnum furcatum* Blume), maple and azalea
Container: Hexagonal vase

Trying to impart the feeling of nature in transition, I caught the energy of the unfurling leaves about to turn into full fledged leaves. Without restraint I arranged the material boldly within the wide-mouthed vase.

Material: *Murasaki-yashio* azalea (*Rhododendron albrechtii* Maxim.) and kerria (*Kerria japonica* DC.)
Container: Old blue and white porcelain vase with ears

Murasaki-yashio azalea, with its gentle, crimson flowers, can be found here and there in the mountains. Surrounded by fresh verdure, they are conspicuously beautiful and eye-pleasing. I arranged them in a narrow-mouthed vase and made the supple branches appear as though they were stretching out with the wind. The golden flowers of the kerria add a bright touch.

Azalea branches break easily. Be careful with them and keep the natural line. It is best to arrange kerria while it is in the bud stage as once in flower, the bloom falls easily.

Material: Agapanthus and common throat-wort (*Trachelium caeruleum* L.)
Container: Glass vase

The agapanthus bears light purple flowers in midsummer, while the throat wort blooms so frailly it seems to drizzle. The combination looks quite modern when arranged *en masse* in this blue glass vase. Some variation was created with the agapanthus leaves.

Material: Spirea thunbergii and rosy lily
Container: Henko-shaped basket

This basket container is about 50 cm (20 inches) in diameter. Let a branch reach out, even a slender one like the spirea thunbergii, to give an impression strong enough to balance the basket. Here I combined the spirea thunbergii with the rosy lily, one of the more delicate members of the lily family.

Material: Azalea (*Enkianthus subsesslilis* Makino), Solomon's seal (*Polygonatum odoratum* Duce) and Japanese spirea (*Spirea japonica* L.)
Container: Bamboo basket

This is a *nageire* style arrangement with the material slanting sideways. After placing a straight line prop across the bamboo cylinder within the basket, I positioned the big, rugged Solomon's seal leaves on the right side, let the reddish brown azalea branches stretch out to the left and placed the red and white Japanese spirea in the center.

Material: Japanese iris, spirea thunbergii, water lily and bulrush
Container: Low basin

I arranged three flowers which grow along the water's edge: the manly iris in the center between the bulrushes and water lilies. With the addition of the fresh green of the spirea thunbergii, an early summer flavor was created.

To arrange the iris, place the flowers in bloom in a higher position and the buds lower. Keep the leaves as they grow naturally to impart a vigorous feeling to the arrangement.

To make the water lilies look as though they were floating on the water, I made the short-cut flowers and the curled leaves stand straight and added floating leaves. A bigger basin allows a better reproduction of natural scenery as the surface of the water can be seen. ▶

Material: Japanese stewartia
Container: Bamboo basket

Belonging to the Theaceae family, this plant blooms in summer with white flowers that are almost transparent. The branches grow straight. To better emphasize the clean beauty of the flowers, I arranged them in a simple, neat way.

Material: Hydrangea
Container: Hand crafted basket

The sight of the heavy, round blooms of hydrangea in shades of blue, purple and pink thrusting above their green leaves during the rainy season is heartwarming. I chose a simple, flat basket for this arrangement. I found one long branch from an old shrub with an amusing shape and let it spread out naturally. Shorter branches form a mass of blooms and foliage for a firm base.

Characteristically, hydrangea does not absorb water well, but cut it in the morning, split the stem and dip it in alcohol and it will drink in water more readily.

Material: False spirea (*Sorbus sorbifolia* A.) and rose
Container: Old Karatsu pot

The false spirea, with its shapely branches, appears cool and refreshing when arranged by itself. The flamboyancy of it in full bloom gives it a Western atmosphere. The addition of two beautiful scarlet roses lends dignity to the arrangement.

Material: Poet's jasmine (*Jasminum officinale* L.) and elegant lily
Container: Modern block-shaped vase

This piece consists of two branches of jasmine and two elegant lilies arranged in an impressive 40 cm (16 inch) wide vase. It is necessary to be careful in selecting the branches as the configuration of each and every small leaf plays an important role when arranging with so few materials. The elegant lily added at the base, brightens the whole arrangement.

Material: Allium, Chilian lily (*Alstroemeria chilensis* Cree.) and statice caspia
Container: Modern vase for *nageire*

In this floral combination, each of the flowers has a distinctly different shape. The star-shaped lily contrasts with the round, lively allium and the small flowers of the statice caspia appear as a mist, softening the atmosphere. The colors in the arrangement go from white to a deep red-purple, almost a maroon.

Material: Blueberry (*Vaccinium oldhami* Miq.), clematis and Solomon's seal (*Polygonatum odoratum* Duce)
Container: Li dynasty vase

I selected branches from an aged blueberry shrub with good lines to suit the dignity of the antique Li dynasty vase. Both branches, which grew parallel, looked tasteful, each in its own way. I was reluctant to remove either one, so I used both. The purple clematis goes well with the fresh green leaves and the Solomon's seal placed at the base gives the arrangement a good overall balance.

Material: Bracken and safflower
Container: Lacquered papier-mache receptacle

Safflower is mentioned in the Man'yo-shu as *Kurenai* (crimson). It has been cultivated since ancient times as dyestuff. Bracken, on the other hand, is known as an edible wild plant. There is something cute about the way bracken raises its flower head from the grass along a mountain path as though signaling the arrival of spring. In summer, however, it grows quite tall and the stems become hard.

As the bracken does not readily absorb water, I positioned them in a *shippo*, a metal holder, rather than a *kenzan*, the needle-point holder.

SUMMER

◀ Material: *Karaito-so* burnet (*Sanguisorba hakusanensis* Makino) and St. John's-wort
Container: Bamboo basket with handle

I arranged the material lightly to make them look as though they were dancing in the wind.

Material: Gladiolus and spike winter hazel (*Corylopsis spicata* Sieb. et Zucc.)
Container: Flat black ceramic vase

Slanting the gladiola in the arrangement gives their sword-shaped leaves a more gentle appearance. The handsome heart-shaped leaves of the spike winter hazel compliment the streamlines of the gladiola.

Material: Fullmoon maple, star of Bethlehem and statice caspia
Container: Ceramic vase for *nageire*

It is not easy to create an effective arrangement in a vase with such striking coloring. Here I complimented the vivid turquoise blue of the vase with the refreshing green of the fullmoon maple, pale orchid toned statice caspia and the snow white star of Bethlehem in a unique combination.

Text on page 130.

Text on page 130.

Text on page 131.

Material: Japanese bulrush and pond lily
Container: Bamboo basket

This arrangement conveys the refreshing atmosphere of the waterside on a summer day. The Japanese bulrush breaks easily in the wind. I suggested a breeze by bending one stalk and gave movement to the arrangement by extending the pond lily leaves in the same direction.

Since the pond lily has the same sponge-like quality as the lotus, it is necessary to pump water into the stems before arranging.

Material: Camellia and white trumpet lily
Container: Aizu vase

The encounters of flowers and containers are always considered, but it is particularly delightful when you find a perfect spot to place the arrangement.

Since it is a narrow-mouthed vase, I allowed the camellia branch to stand straight and took advantage of the side branch at the top. The white trumpet lilies were arranged to the left and in the rear to keep a good balance.

The line of the camellia branch can be fully emphasized by judiciously removing leaves.

▶

SUMMER

Text on page 131.

Text on page 131.

Material: Zebra grass and rose mallow
Container: Bamboo basket with handle

One of Japan's typical summer flowers, the rose mallow blooms profusely on spreading branches under the blazing summer sun.

For this cool-looking arrangement, I used a single flower in half bloom and the zebra grass in a rather large basket.

The rose mallow does not absorb water easily. Pick them early in the morning, dip the stem ends in hot water for two or three minutes and then soak them in deep water for a long time before arranging.

Material: Pine and showy lily
Container: Big pot

With the entry of an old brick warehouse in the strong midsummer sun as the setting, I sprinkled cold water around for a cooling effect and the pine and lily positioned in the big old pot added a lively touch. ▶

Material: *Ko-amacha* hydrangea (*Hydrangea macrophylla* Ser.) and Chinese bellflower
Container: Flat basket

This hydrangea, similar to the wild hydrangea, is blue when it first comes out, but gradually turns pink. For this arrangement, I added some Chinese bellflowers nearly the same color, some quite short. The longer one I slanted in low.

Material: Scabious pincushion (*Scabiosa japonica* Miq.) and white burnet (*Sanguisorba albiflora* Makino)
Container: Flat basket

The Japanese scabious is a biennial grass which grows in sunny places on mountains and highlands. Its big, light purple flowers are striking. The seed pods formed after the flowers have bloomed, are unique in shape, reminiscent of close-cropped heads.

The white flowered burnet grows on rocks and cliffs high in the mountains in cold climates. I arranged the rare, white burnet in a high position and placed the scabious in the front, long and slanted.

Material: Chinese monkshood, prairie gentian, purple meadow rue, snow-on-the-mountain (*Euphorbia marginata* Pursh) and amethyst eryngo or sea holly (*Eryngium amethystium* L.)
Container: Cylindrical ceramic vase

I arranged the light purple flowers in this white, slender vase to suggest the bracing air of early autumn.

The snow-on-the-mountain originally came from North America. The edges of the leaves turn white in summer. The prairie gentian also came North America and belongs to the gentian family. Variegated prairie gentian have recently been cultivated. The purple meadow rue is a rare flower in Japan, its purple calyces and yellow anthers form a beautiful flower. The Chinese monkshood grows in a variety of types, each slightly different from the other depending upon where they grow.

Material: Mountain ash (*Sorbus commixta* Hedl.) and yellow chrysanthemum
Container: Old Bizen pot

The leaves of the mountain ash start to turn red early, making it a harbinger of autumn.

This branch was large and shapeless, without any character. By cutting off sprigs and removing thick leaves one by one, I uncovered the branch surface to better define the line.

As the massive old Bizen pot is an integral part of the composition, I used only yellow chrysanthemums to complete the arrangement.

Text on page 131.

Text on page 131.

Material: Elephant's ear (*Begonia evansiana* Andrews) and Chinese miscanthus
Container: Bamboo basket with side handle

It is soothing to find elephant's ear begonia in a damp corner of the garden beginning to put forth tender, pale crimson flowers. It makes you forget the heat of the summer for the moment.

The elephant's ear flowers appear all the prettier when arranged in a basket with the big, dewy leaves in the background and stalks of tall Chinese miscanthus just starting to turn red.

The elephant's ear is also suited to Western containers such as glassware. Bear in mind that the leaves of the begonia, which make the flowers stand out, play an important role in the arrangement.

Material: *Tsukubane* buckleya (*Buckleya Joan* Makino) and Japanese spirea (*Spiraea japonica* L.)
Container: Vase for *nageire*

The *tsukubane* bears inconspicuous, light green flowerets in early summer, but when autumn comes, the seed pods appear like little shuttlecocks from behind the leaves, without our noticing. When arranging the *tsukubane*, be sure to remove quite a few leaves to better show the pods.

Material: Chinese bellflower, patrinia (*Patrinia scabiosaefolia* Link.) and pampas grass (*Themeda japonica* Tanaka)
Container: Sennari-shaped bamboo basket

I selected charming and innocent looking flowers, the patrinia and Chinese bellflowers, to match the gentleness of the newly emerged pampas grass.

When using a basket with a handle, arrange the material in front of the handle. In doing so, the arrangement reaches out to the front, conveying a tender sentiment.

Material: Tree clethra (*Clethra barbinervis* Sieb. et Zucc.) and *iwa-giku* chrysanthemum
Container: Modern ceramic vase

I kept the material long in this vase which widens at the bottom, to emphasize the importance of the big, colored leaves and interesting branches of the tree clethra as they reach out to the left.

The *iwa-giku* chrysanthemum grows in rocky places in the mountains of Japan and China. One flower blooms from each of its slender stems and the leaves are small and lovely. I massed about twenty of them in a bundle and let them lean gently against the powerful clethra branches for a pert, cute touch.

Material: Fullmoon maple, Japanese white bush clover (*Lespedeza bicolor* Turcz.) and *yuga-giku* (*Aster pinnatifidus* Makino)
Container: Bamboo winnowing basket

The splendor of the fullmoon maple turning red in such a remarkably beautiful way in the crisp autumn makes it the king of all maples.

The white flowered Japanese bush clover is also called *koborehagi*, fallen bush clover, because the flowers fall one after another in a sad, but appealing way.

This piece represents the beauty of the transitory lives of flowers, trying their best to look as glamorous as possible, knowing they will soon be gone.

Material: Azalea (*Enkianthus subsesslilis* Makino) and gentian
Container: Copper vase with snowflake pattern

I placed an antique copper vase against a *shoin*-style *shoji*, paper sliding door. The gentian leaves, which have turned crimson, and the red azalea leaves express the afterglow of fall.

I arranged all three gentians on the right side to better emphasize the line of the azalea as it reaches out to the left. In arranging materials of similar shade, position one slightly apart from the other. It helps the piece look neat and orderly. Consider the straight lines of the *shoji* frame in the background as part of the arrangement and do not remove too many leaves from the azalea branch.

Material: Red-veined maple, chestnut, Japanese toad-lily (*Tricyrtis hirta* Hook), plantain lily (*Hosta undulata* Bailey) and *nodake* (*Peucedanum decursivum* Maxim.)
Container: Bamboo basket

The autumn leaves of various trees and shrubs look bright and beautiful on the mountainside and in fields where the air is clear and cool. The leaves of the plantain lily had turned yellow in the chilly air and I was fascinated by their subdued shade. Yielding to their temptation, I arranged an armful in a vegetable basket. It may be because I arranged all of the autumn leaves low, forming a base, that the piece has a somewhat cheerful touch, although the overall arrangement creates a quiet atmosphere. The chestnuts and the *nodake* are the only material positioned on a *kenzan*, needlepoint holder. The rest are arranged in the *nageire* style, in a light manner.

Material: Bittersweet and gentian
Container: Bamboo strainer

In late autumn, the leaves of the bittersweet fall and the seed pods burst open to reveal the red berries inside.

Take full advantage of the shape of the vines and make an amusing arrangement. Instead of the usual *nageire* vase, use your bamboo strainer, readily at hand.

Material: Rabbit-ear iris (Iris laevigata Fischer), reed and lotus
Container: Rectangular basin

The tips of the rabbit-ear iris leaves turn yellowish in the late autumn and the lotus leaves give a strong impression of the season. The light pink lotus petals of summer are gone and the seed pod that takes its place almost looks like a honeycomb. The colors of the withered leaves show the subtle change from autumn to winter. By incorporating them in an arrangement, you can almost feel the movement of the earth rather than just suggesting a seasonal change.

Material: Japanese witch hazel (*Hamamelis japonica* Sieb. et Zucc.), *kaji-ichigo* (*Rubus trifidus* Thunb.) and Chinese miscanthus
Container: Tall rectangular vase

The combination of the exhilarating red Japanese witch hazel leaves, the yellow-green leaves of the *kaji-ichigo* and the Chinese miscanthus turned red arranged in this modern vase is tastefully dramatic.

The straight, long lines of the miscanthus, so typical of the fields in autumn, give a cheerful note to the arrangement.

Material: *Daikagura* camellia
Container: Modern, narrow necked vase

To emphasize the beauty of the leaves, I used but a single flower in this Western vase.

The leaves of the *daikagura* are variegated and the flowers are elegant. Although I used quite a few leaves here in a mass, I also allowed some of the branches to show. I tried to imagine the way the flower would bloom while I was arranging this piece. The arrangement looks as though the branches were just tied together. It doesn't happen that way. Select and position your branches carefully and adjust the leaves for a good composition.

Material: Japanese red pine, spray mum and leucothoe (*Leucothoe grayana* Maxim.)
Container: Tall, cylindrical ceramic vase

The spray mum is material with a Western appearance and a light touch. Its flowers spread out from the ends of the branches. In combination with the Japanese red pine, this arrangement would be quite at home in a room of Western decor.

Material: Cymbidium, baby's breath and tara vine (*Actinida arguta* Planch.)
Container: Low basin

The tara vine is referred to as red vine because of its red stems. The interesting curves of its vines make it excellent material for an arrangement.

I cut one stalk of cymbidium into three parts, placed it low in the arrangement and encircled it with baby's breath to cover the *kenzan*.

Material: Japanese winterberry and white chrysanthemum
Container: Sue pot by Moritoshi Tokuzawa

The Japanese winterberry, when the berries ripe, provides bright color in a season when not many materials are available, from late autumn through early winter. I arranged it with white chrysanthemums in a Sue pot. Since it is a wide-mouthed vase, I decided to let a long branch of the winterberry soar to the left and arrange the chrysanthemums low in the container to create a sense of stability.

Treat the Japanese winterberry carefully for the branches break easily and the berries fall. Accentuate the arrangement by taking advantage of the natural shape of the branches.

Text on page 132.

WINTER

Material: *Yuzu* citron and *Saga* chrysanthemum
Container: Narrow-necked bronze vase

The *yuzu* citron fruit is indispensable for Japanese cuisine. The elegance of this ripe fruit as it hangs from the branch among the leaves, is exquisite. To compliment the shapely citron branch, I added quite a few Saga chrysanthemums. It gives a cheerful touch.

The fruit laden branch is heavier than it appears. To counterbalance it, I added another long branch to reach the bottom of the vase.

Material: Japanese beautyberry (*Callicarpa dichotoma* Raeus.) and small chrysanthemum
Container: Round three-mouthed vase

I combined branches with their colorful clusters of small purple berries with small flowered chrysanthemums and arranged them in this unusual vase.

The container has three openings. I let a branch of beautyberry reach out from the lowest opening, giving full play to the natural curves of the material. The small chrysanthemums with a profusion of little leaves were garden grown.

Text on page 132.

PART II

WILD FLOWERS & CREATIVE WORK

Material: Stauntonia (*Stauntonia hexaphylla* Decne.) and red star lily
Container: Bamboo (Ichiju-giri)

The stauntonia is evergreen and, as it bears clusters of three, five or seven leaves, is considered to be auspicious by the Japanese and is often planted in gardens. The way the tips of the slender vine grow like tendrils is fascinating.

The stauntonia in this arrangement has not yet flowered. The cinnabar red star lily seems to be demonstrating its remarkable beauty. The hanging bamboo container gives this arrangement the feeling of one used for tea ceremony.

Material: *Nazuna* Shepherd's purse (*Capsella burse-pastoris* Medicus), dandelion, horsetail (*Equisetum arvense* L.) and field horsetail
Container: *Masu*, (a Japanese measure)

These wild herbs, *nazuna*, dandelions, horsetails and field horsetails, can be seen anywhere. Clustered together in a small measuring box, they take on a special charm and convey the warmth of spring.

Since wild flowers do not absorb water easily, I used a *shippo* holder instead of the needle-pointed *kenzan*.

Material: Chinese linden tree (*Tilia miqueliana* Maxim.) and skunk cabbage (*Symplocarpus renifilius* Schott)
Container: Bizen basin

Belongs to the tiliaceae family. Native to China, the tall, deciduous linden tree is very unique. Related to the Indian Bo tree (ficus religiosa: moraceae), where it is remarkable for its longevity and great size, it is sacred to Buddhists and is often planted in temples grounds.

The leaves of the linden look like distorted triangles. As floral material, its major characteristic is the leaf shape at the time of flowering.

The skunk cabbage grows wild in damp regions. The Japanese call this particular type *zazen-sō* because the brown spathe surrounding the head looks like a priest preforming Zen meditation.

As both materials are associated with the Buddha, I tried to arrange them with a serene, meditative mind.

Material: *Uwamizu* cherry (*Prunus grayana* Maxim.)
Container: Basket

The *Prunus grayana*, belonging to the cherry genus of the rosae family, is a tall deciduous tree with ear-like white blossoms. These trees can be found in full bloom with faintly fragrant blossoms in both mountains and fields in April and May.

As there are few bends in the branches, as floral material they lack character. I removed some leaves to reveal parts of the branches. I also pruned some of the blossoms to better appreciate those remaining. Since this is rare ikebana material, I arranged it by itself, big and soft.

Material: Maule's quince (*Chaenomeles maulei* Schneid.) and Rodger's bronze-leaf (*Rodegersia podophylla* A. Gray)
Container: Modern ceramic vase

When you walk along a mountain path, if you're lucky you might come upon a maule's quince in bloom with plump, crimson buds. or, on the edge of a mountain stream, a magnificent stand of Rodger's bronze-leaf might catch your eye.

I combined these two with the slender branches of the quince spreading out from the container while the cornflowers stand high and generous.

Material: Greenbrier and fan columbine (*Aquilegia flabellata* Sieb. et Zucc.)
Container: Karatsu vase with ears

This *nageire* style is created with a harmonious arrangement of a shapely greenbrier branch and two purple columbine flowers.

◀ Material: Flowering crab-apple (*Malus Tschonoskii* Schneid.) and Japanese wake-robin (*Trillium japonicum* Matsum.)
Container: Antique square-mouthed copper vase

The flowering crab-apple puts forth crimson buds which turn into white blossoms. The backs of the leaves are covered with whitish hair.

The Japanese name for wake-robin, *kinugasa-sō*, comes from its verticillated leaves which somehow resemble the silk umbrellas used for the processions of noblemen in the Nara period. Each branch bears a single flower and each flower has great dignity. I have chosen this antique vessel as a fitting compliment to the flower.

Material: *Ikari-sō* barrenwort (*Epimedium grandiflorum* Morr.)
Container: Celadon brazier

◀ The Japanese call this plant *ikari-sō*, meaning anchor grass, as the shape of the flowers resembles a ship's anchor. Each branch bears three leaves. The color of the flowers varies from white to crimson and the shape is quite unique. The amusing container adds a humorous touch to this spring arrangement.

Material: *Miyama-hanshōzuru* clematis (*Clematis alpine* Mill.) and black or kamchatka lily (*Fritillaria camtschatcensis* Ker-Gawl)
Container: Basket

The *miyama-hanshōzuru* clematis bloom in shadowy copses. Almost hidden, they twine around trees. The pretty little flowers look like lovely pink bells. When arranging, remove some of the leaves of the vine. When working with a creeper for ikebana, it is necessary to twine it around a branch. As I used a basket for the container, it was necessary to make the branch as inconspicuous as possible.

The black lily does not absorb water well and so I arranged it with the root, after rinsing the soil away.

Text on page 132.

Text on page 132.

Material: Blueberry (*Vaccinium oldhami* Miq.) and *kurin-sō* (*Primula japonica* A. Gray)
Container: Winnowing basket

The blueberry used in this arrangement grows in the uplands near the Garden of Man'yo where plants mentioned in that anthology are grown one thousand meters above sea level. As this particular branch is shapely and the leaves are small, I thought it better to arrange just this single branch. I supported the *kurin-sō* with a *shippo* as though it simply sits there.

Material: *Tebako-momijigasa* (*Cacalia tebakoensis* Makino) and *yama-hotarubukuro* bellflower (*Campanula punctata* Lam.)
Container: Gourd-shaped basket

I wished to arrange the *tebako-momijigasa* and the bellflower in a gourd-shaped basket for an early summer tea ceremony. In picking material to go with something like the *tebako-momijigasa*, which has inconspicuous flowers and distinctive leaves, be well-advised to choose one that neither competes with nor destroys the beauty of the leaves. ▶

Material: Clintonis (*Clintonia udensis* Trautv. et Mey) and *otome* lily or rosy lily
Container: Kiseto basin

The clintonis, also called Clinton's lily, a genus of perennial herbs (family Liliaceae) has lovely little white flowers in early summer. Its ovate leave grow big after the flowers have bloomed. As it goes to seed, the indigo blue berries and the large leaves give a sophisticated atmosphere rather than the wild grass it is.

The *otome* (maiden) lily is also called *himesayuri* (small, pretty). The way they flower can be likened to the modern, flamboyant girls of today.

Material: *Kurumaba-tsukubane-sō* herb-Paris (*Paris verticillata* M. v. Bieb.) and Japanese spirea (*Spiraea japonica* L.)
Container: Basket with handle

Of the many wild plants of summer, there is something neat and quiet about herb-Paris that is very appealing. I arranged two stalks at differing heights and angles and placed the Japanese spirea so they would modestly peek out from the back.

Text on page 133.

Material: *Shirane-aoi* mallow (*Glaucidium palmatum* Sieb. et Zucc.), *sanzun* iris and yellow violet (*Viola brevistipulata* W. Becker)
Container: Square basket

I have always longed to see the light purple, dreamlike flowers of the *shirane-aoi*. Mr. Onodera of the Garden of Man'yo where these rare plants are cultivated today, kindly brought them to me along with the yellow violets that he had grown. I tied all of the violets in a bundle with a rubber band and placed them at the foot of the *shirane-aoi*. I used a *shippo* instead of a *kenzan* to hold the material.

Material: Solomon's seal (*Polygonatum falcatum* A. Gray), wake-robin (*Trillium smallii* Maxim.), Japanese spirea (*Spiraea japonica* L.), golden-banded lily and *tsukubane-sō* (*Paris tetraphylla* A. Gray)
Container: Basket with a 70 cm (28″) diameter

In this arrangement of five wild plants, I gave the Solomon's seal the leading role as it was such a beauty, large with many fine flowers. I placed the gold-banded lily and the Japanese spirea low in the basket.

Material: *Tekiri-suge* sedge (*Carex kiotensis* Franch. et Sav.), Siberian yarrow (*Achillae sibirica* Ledeb.) and *tsukubane-sō* herb-Paris (*Paris tetraphylla* A. Gray)
Container: Bamboo basket

The Japanese names for sedge and yarrow mean cut and saw, rather rude names for floral material. The first earned the name because it is easy to cut fingers while handling and the second because of the saw-toothed leaves. Sometimes flower names are too precise. These names certainly don't fit after they are arranged.

Material: Green barley (*Hordeum vulgare* L.) and *sawa-oguruma* starwort (*Senecio pierotti* Miq.)
Container: Basket

The *sawa-oruruma* is a bright, happy-looking starwort which grows on damp plains with plenty of sunshine. I placed a rather tall container inside a basket normally used at farmhouses and arranged the barley *nageire* style. If you arrange each barley separately, they would lean to one side so it is advisable to tie them together. A casual arrangement seems to suit a rustic basket.

Material: *Gamazumi* viburnum (*Viburnum dilatatum* Thunb.), *shiran* (*Bletilla striata* Reichb. fil.)
Container: Basket with handle

The viburnum, which bears little, white corymbose flowers on the tips of sprigs in the summer, produces bright red berries in the autumn.

The *shiran* is a wild orchid which grows on damp plains and on cliffs. I arranged one single branch of the viburnum in a basket with a handle after removing some of the leaves to give it a light atmosphere. When positioning the *shiran*, pay attention to the angles of the leaves as they too play an important role.

Text on page 133.

Material: *Uguisu-kagura* honeysuckle (*Lonicera gracilipes* Miq.), Indian turnip (*Arisaema sikokianum* Franch. et Sav.) and *nirin-sō* (*Anemone flaccida* Fr. Schm.)
Container: Oblong basket

In this oval basket, I tried to reproduce a mountain path in early summer using three kinds of plants with differing characteristics.

Material: *Mizu-chidori* (*Platanthera hologlottis* Maxim.) and *mizu-giku* (*Inula ciliaris* Maxim.)
Container: Narrow necked flower vase

In arranging wild plants, you can use either a number of different kinds, or limit yourself to two or three. In both cases, you can make a fine arrangement. However, when using *mizu-chidori*, which has a refreshing appearance, an arrangement with just a few pieces would be more effective and create a surprisingly modern impression. The bright yellow color of the *mizu-giku* successfully firms up the composition, giving good balance for the heavy white flowered spikes. The combination is sharp and pleasing.

Material: *Noriutsugi* (*Hydrangea paniculata* Sieb.)
Container: Small vase atop a footed *aizu* lacquered, individual Japanese table

The small lacquered table fits well with the color of this traditional *shoin*-style room. The pure white flowers and green leaves are a strong accent in beautiful contrast. I feel that it is most effective to arrange the *noriutsugi* by itself as the green leaves are as big and impressive as the flowers.

Material: Day lily (*Hemerocallis fulva* L.)
Container: Basket with handle

The day lily, growing at the edge of ditches in the fields, rice paddies or on river banks, reaches a height of about a meter. Often I would come across the day lily here and there when I was a small child. I decided to arrange it by itself to keep the simple beauty of the flowers intact.

Material: *Sankaku-i* bulrush (*Scirpus triqueter* L.) and *Tamagawa* toad-lily (*Tricytris latifolia* Maxim.)
Container: Flat, round basket

I arranged some of the *sankaku-i* bulrush high and others lower to create some rhythm to this work and added the toad lily with its dark green leaves at the base. Together in the basket of an open-weave, they make a refreshing combination. ▶

◀ Material: *Kugai-sō* (*Veronicastrum sibiricum Pennell) and Siebold compion* (*Lychnis sieboldi* v. Houtt)
Container: Black oribe lipped bowl

The *kugai-sō* grows in sunny, grassy regions of the mountains to a height of about one meter and blooms with pretty, purple flowered spikes.

I positioned the *kugai-sō* high so the bending ears show to good advantage and then arranged the campion low and small at the base.

Material: Common spiderwort (*Tradescantia virginiana* L.) ▶
Container: Small container within a basket lid

Quite a few kinds of spiderwort are available for planting in the garden in a choice of flower colors, white, blue, red or pink. The flowers only last one day, but it is fascinating to see new flowers appear one after another every morning, blooming quietly, awakening to the morning dew.

For this arrangement, I used only spiderwort, positioning the five pieces to give full view of the refined white flowers and the shape of the slender leaves.

Material: Willow herb (*Epilobium angustifolium* L.) and chethra loosestrife (*Lysimachia clethroides* Duby)
Container: Basket

It is overwhelming to catch sight of colonies of bright pink flowers.

I arranged the willow herb high as seen in the mid-summer fields, taking full advantage of the straight and prim stems. I placed the clethra loosestrife with its casual curves and bends low at the base. I tried to make the overall impression warm and cheerful.

Material: Siebold campion (*Lychnis sieboldi* v. Houtt), patrinia (*Patrinia scabiosaefolia* Link.), pampas grass (*Themeda japonica* Tanaka), *okera* (*Atractylis ovata* Thunb.), *chidakesashi* (*Astilbe microphylla* Knoll), super pink (*Dianthus superbus* L.) and rose of sharon (*Hibiscus syriacus* L.)
Container: Bamboo basket with handle

I created a cheerful arrangement of seven summer flowers in a rather large basket with a handle. This type of pampas grass looks more graceful than others, the downy hair on its slender leaves makes it appear even more gentle.

Fascinatingly elegant as it is, the rose of Sharon lives a fleeting life of just one day.

When using several types of material in one arrangement, determine how it should look beforehand, then start arranging from the front, allowing a moderate distance between each piece.

Material: Patrinia (*Patrinia scabiosaefolia* Link.), bush clover (*Lespedeza cyrtobotrya* Miq.), Japanese bellflower, water hemlock (*Cicuta virosa* L.), super pink (*Dianthus superbus* L.), Japanese boneset (*Eupatorium japonicum* Thunb.), safflower (*Carthamus tinctorius* L.), Japanese iris (*Iris ensata* Thunb.) and cockscomb
Container: basket

People who lived in ancient times must have picked the many wild flowers of midsummer and arranged them much as we do today.

The mountain and field scenery of the good old days is hard to find in these times and yet it keeps coming back to me. This arrangement represents the beautiful bounty of summer.

Material: *Me-takarako* (*Ligularia stenocephala* Matsumura et Koidz.) and *Tamagawa* toad-lily (*Tricytris latifolia* Maxim.)
Container: Low, round backet

Within this low basket, I combined the *me-takarako*, which grows in the cool, dusky thickets of the forests, with the *Tamagawa* toad lily, which blooms in mountainous districts. They may not be combined in nature's own pattern, but these two different yellow flowers complement each other for a quiet, graceful arrangement.

Material: Chinese miscanthus, great burnet (*Sanguisorba officinalis* L.), meadow rue (*Thalictrum minus* L.), patrinia (*P. scabiosaefolia* Link.), common goldenrod (*Solidago virga-aurea* L.) clethra loosestrife (*Lysimachia clethroides* Duby), *sawa-hiyodori* (*Eupatorium lindleyanum* DC.), *miyako* thistle (*Saussurea maximowiczii* Herd.), common yellow loosestrife (*Lysimachia vulgaris* L.), and *hime-higotai* (*Saussurea pulchella* Fisch.)
Container: Basket

When the winds bring a chill to the country, the Chinese miscanthus attracts our attention in the fields and highlands. But, search carefully and you will find a wealth of flowering plants such as great burnets, gentians and super pinks hiding underneath the Chinese miscanthus. ▶

Text on page 133.

Text on page 133.

Material: *Katsura* tree (*Cercidiphyllum japonicum* Sieb. et Zucc.) and Japanese boneset (*Eupatorium japonicum* Thunb.)
Container: Karatsu pot

As far as line and character go, the *katsura* tree is not such elegant material, but it does have an irresistible charm. A bit of contrivance, such as removing some leaves, helps generate a warm touch.

Material: Chinese miscanthus, common yellow loosestrife (*Lysimachia vulgaris* L.), yellow stone crop (*Sedum kamtschaticum* Fisch.), Japanese meadowsweet (*Filipendula purpurea* Maxim.), white Japanese spirea (*Spiraea japonica* L. f.), *okera* (*Atractylis ovata* Thunb.), and Japanese astilbe (*Astilbe odontophylla* Miq.)
Container: Basket with handle

This particular Japanese miscanthus reaches this stage in early autumn, still retaining the youthfulness of summer. It gives a more powerful impression than those waving silvery hands to the sunshine.

I gathered wild plants decorating the fields in early autumn for this arrangement in a basket.

Material: Chinese miscanthus, kudzu-vine (*Pueraria Thunbergiana* Benth.), bush clover (*Lespedeza cyrotobotrya* Miq.), patrinia (*P. scabiosaefolia* Link.), super pink (*Dianthus superbus* L.), *sawa-hiyodori* (*Eupatorium lindleyanum* DC.) and the Japanese bellflower gone to seed.
Container: Basket with handle

It is quite difficult to gather all of the flowers that come into bloom between summer and fall. I made a pleasant arrangement of seven kinds of autumn flowers after the well known seven flower (*nanakusa*) by Yamanoue-no-Okura, a poet whose poems are included in "*Man'yo-shu*".

Material: *Otoko-yōzome* (*Viburnum phlobatrichum* Sieb. et Zucc.) and toad lily (*Tricyrtis japonica* Miq.)
Container: Kiseto water pot

By positioning a long branch of *otoko-yozōme* viburnum with berries and sparse leaves so it slants to the left, and then placing a branch with beautiful autumn leaves in the front, this piece makes a colorful *nageire* arrangement. I then added three pieces of toad lily in the middle.

Material: Lobelia (*L. sessilifolia* Lamb.), gentian and *yama-shirogiku* (*Aster ageratoides* Turcz.)
Container: Tall, open weave basket

◀ Lobelia, with deep purple flowers on a meter-long stalk, is found in damp areas of the fields and mountains. By late autumn, the gentle flowers turn to hard seed pods.

I used a rustic basket for this arrangement of lobelia stalks that had turned different colors. The gentian and *yama-shirogiku* add to the feeling of autumn.

Material: *Amanyu* angelica (*Angelica edulis* Miyabe), nerine japonica (*Lycoris radiata* Herb.) and bracken (*Pteridium aquilinum* L.)
Container: Ceramic bowl

I combined the white angelica flowers which look as though they were made of lace, with the red flowers of the nerine japonica. To create an autumn atmosphere, I added bracken leaves which had turned golden and placed them low in the arrangement. Since the leaves of the angelica are quite big and tend to droop, I removed them and let only the interesting features of the flowers and stems show to good advantage. ▶

Material: *Karahana-sō* hops (*Humulus lupulus* L.), Oriental bittersweet and monkshood (*Aconitum japonicum* Thunb.)
Container: *Nageire* vase

Karahana-sō belongs to the hop family. It's a climbing plant that grows thickly around trees on mountains and in the fields. Since it does not stand firmly by itself, I used the bittersweet as a support. You can make interesting arrangements with hops in either a tall vase or in a hanging vase, using one or two vines.

Material: Japanese *udo* salad (*Aralia cordata* Thunb.) and mountain ash (*Sorbus gracilis* K. Koch)
Container: Glass vase

In a reddish-brown glass vase, I arranged *udo* with berries of a similar color. I enjoy this material, it makes me think of Japanese toy fireworks. The one leaf is a needed accent. ▶

Material: Japanese spirea (*Spiraea betulifolia* Pall.) and common goldenrod (*Solidago virga-aurea* L.)
Container: Two-mouthed, modern ceramic compote

I arranged Japanese spirea in *nageire* style in this modern compote to give full play to the deep color and its lovely, round leaves. Accented with the common goldenrod, the piece looks neat and refreshing.

Material: White peony (*Paeonia japonica* Miyabe et Takeda) and *yūga-giku* (*Aster pinnatifidus* Bunge.)
Container: Basket

The white peony takes quite a few years to grow quietly under the trees in fields and mountains and finally it blooms with white flowers. When the flowers are gone, the seed pods develop in a striking combination of red and black.

The leaves of this particular wild peony have big worm eaten holes, but I liked the shape of the branch. It looks like a man with outstretched arms. The *yūga-giku* bloom in a spray at the end of a stalk, making them look very lively. In this work, only two pieces were used.

Material: Plume poppy (*Macleya cordata* R. Br.), *oyama-bokuchi* thistle (*Synurus pungens* Kitam.), golden-banded lily, clethra loosestrife (*Lysimachia clethroides* Duby) and *okera* (*Atractylis ovata* thunb.)
Container: Basket

The plume poppy can be found even in urban areas, in vacant lots and on the banks of train tracks. It is a poisonous plant which oozes a yellowish-red latex from the stems.

The *oyama-bokuchi* looks very much like the thistle. It grows in the grassy plains and bears big, heavy looking flowers on remarkably tall and strong stems.

No matter how many of these wild plant materials I put together, there is a mysterious charm to the natural shapes and colors whether they grow in fields or mountains and they never interfere or detract one from the other.

Material: Wild grapevine (*Vitis coignetiae* Pulliat)
Container: Open weave flat basket

The dynamic wild grapevine spreads its vines from one tree to another. the leaves are big and autumn colors each leaf differently one by one until few green leaves remain. I left one green leaf in the arrangement as an accent. In using longer vines, remove some of the leaves to let the line of the vine show. This gives a vigorous touch to the piece.

Material: Bog billberry (*Vaccinum uliginosum* L.), grass of Parnassus (*Parnassia palustris* L.), club-moss (*Lycopodium serratum* Thunb.) and *koke-otogiri* St. John's wort (*Hypericum laxum* Thunb.)
Container: Free form *moribana* container

In this piece, the brown basin is likened to a tray with a smaller container at the curve of the right side. I positioned a branch of the bog billberry so it extended to the far left and beyond the confines of the brown container and then gathered small wild plants at its base. The distinct white grass of Parnassus and the tiny red leaves of *koke-otogiri* add interest. ▶

Material: *Ogi* common reed (*Miscanthus sacchariflorus* Blenth. et Hook L.), osmund (*Osmundastrum cinnamomeum* L.), *sawa-hiyodori* (*Eupatorium Lindleyanum* DC.), wormwood (*Artemisia vulgaris* L.) and *kuma-sasa* (*Sasa albo-marginata* Makino et Sibata)
Container: Basket with handle

I have gathered subdued-colored flowers and plants found in fields and mountains in the late autumn. ▶

AUTUMN

◀ Material: Pampas grass (*Themeda japonica* Tanaka), oil grass, *oyama-bokuchi* (*Synurus pungens* Kitam.), *shirane-aoi* mallow leaves (*Glaucidium palmatum* Sieb. et Zucc.) and common yellow loosestrife (*Lysimachia vulgaris* L.)
Container: Sue pot

The ears of the pampas grass are starting to come out and its leaves form light, gentle arcs. The flowers of the *shirane-aoi* are light purple and beautiful in early summer. Seeing its leaves turning yellow like this makes me feel the chilly mountain air of late autumn.

Material: *Yuki-zasa* star flowered lily of the valley (*Smilacina japonica* A. Gray) and wheel lily (*Lilium medeoloides* A. Gray) ▶
Container: Winnowing basket

I arranged the wheel lily with its dark brown seed pods in a slanting upright position and low in the front I placed two pieces of *yuki-zasa* with its bright red berries hanging down. In the rear, I placed another piece of *yuki-zasa* slightly higher. I left enough space to clearly show the worm-eaten leaves that had turned yellow, to better identify the atmosphere of autumn.

Material: Japanese witch hazel (*Hamamelis japonica* Sieb. et Zucc.) and cinquefoil (*Potentilla recta*)
Container: Folkcraft basket

The Japanese witch hazel bears four-petaled flowers that look like twisted, yellow ribbons in early spring. The leaves grow thickly in the summer and then begin to change color at the end of the summer. Around that time seed pods develop, a definite sign of autumn. I tried to demonstrate in a simple basket a sense of the season going from summer to autumn.

Material: Mountain maple, *kuma-sasa* (*Sasa albo-marginata* Makino et Shibata) and gentian
Container: Rectangular ceramic

I arranged two or three gentians modestly in the midst of this gorgeous array of colored leaves. The edges of the low *kuma-sasa* have already started turning white, heralding the arrival of winter.

Material: Chinese miscanthus, fullmoon maple and red star lily
Container: Basket

Chinese miscanthus and fullmoon maple is a typical combination for autumn arrangements. Here I added the lovely red star lily as a poignant reminder of summer. ▶

Material: Azalea (*Enkianthus subsessillis* Makino), Chinese miscanthus, patrinia (Patrinia scabiosaefolia Link.), gentian, common goldenrod (*Solidago virga-aurea* L.), great burnet (*Sanguisorba officinalis* L.) and *gamazumi* viburnum (*V. Dilatatum* Thunb.)
Container: Receptacle for steamed rice with red beans

This is a large, colorful piece with the colored leaves of the *azalea* and berries of the viburnum as the main materials.
The green leaves of the viburnum and the purple flowers of the gentian, though not conspicuous, successfully firm up the whole arrangement.

PART III

IKEBANA: KOZAN SCHOOL

The Characteristics of the Kozan School

"ARRANGE PLUM TREES LIKE PLUM TREES AND PEACH TREES LIKE PEACH TREES."

The ikebana of Kozan was revolutionary when the school was founded. "*Jiyuuka*" was completely different than the stylized *kakubana* (*rikka* or *seika*) of those Meiji days. Kozan philosophy is to capture the natural forms of plants as nature formed them and arrange them freely and comfortably.

The major tenet of the Kozan school is to arrange material naturally, to value the individuality of each plant and make use its characteristics. That does not mean that plants picked in the fields should be put into containers as they are. It does mean to arrange flowers in a way that makes them look as lively and vivacious in containers as they are in their natural surroundings.

Another objective of the school is to take advantage of the natural shape of a branch without making rules or forms the primary concern. The foremost rule is to keep the vigor and natural charm of the plants intact.

The meaning of the precept, "Arrange plum trees like plum trees and peach trees like peach trees," is to value the natural characteristics of each plant and to fully understand the role of each flower, each branch and each leaf in arranging the material. The angular branches of the plum tree have completely different features from the soft curves of the peach.

Even a seemingly ordinary flower has a characteristic peculiar to that plant. If the shape of a branch is not satisfactory, find the salient point of that plant material and concentrate on it. Study the shape of the leaves, the pleasing color, the delicacy of a single flower or the effect of a cluster. Floral material can look more distinctive in a container than when blooming in its natural element only if you extract the characteristic indigenous to the plant. What you choose to emphasize reveals your preference, and gives clue to your individuality. The arranger makes a personal statement of discernment and attitude in ikebana.

In today's world, with options of environment and lifestyle readily available, it is highly significant to be individualistic. In singling out a particular aspect of the plant material, a related trait of the arranger fuses to make an ikebana arrangement an art piece.

Consideration for the Four Seasons

It is regretable that there is less and less of a sense of the seasons today, partially due to the variety of floral material available throughout the year. Plants growing in the Japanese climate show subtle changes from one season to another. Incorporate these changes of season in your ikebana and your arrangements will express the vigor of early spring, the beauty of flowers in full bloom or the nostalgia of a turning leaf. Ikebana must not be a mere decoration, it must signify the season or the changing of the seasons.

The founder, Kozan Okada I was fascinated by the changes in iris through the seasons. He became familiar with the characteristics of each segment of the plant and every nuance in its life cycle. His study was a lifelong quest. His arrangements were made with love and understanding.

Handling Flower Material

It is important to handle flowers with affection. When holding a flower, hold the stem between the leaves so not to bruise the thin petals or damage the foliage. When you put a flower down, place it gently from the top to the bottom, as if caressing it. This way, neither the flowers nor the leaves will be harmed.

When you take the flower material home after a lesson, water the back of the leaves. Place the stem ends of each type used together and wrap each separately in newspaper. Finally wrap them all together in the flower wrapper.

At home, remove the flowers from their wrappings and soak all of the material in deep water before arranging. Flowers tend to wilt on the way home in the summertime, but in any season they are out of water in transit.

The Combinations of Materials

In the early years of the Kozan School, the arrangements were a simple combination of two or three kinds of material. The exception was in autumn when five or seven different kinds were used.

Changes in lifestyle have also influenced ikebana in color sense and the feeling of space and volume. Today we have more diverse combinations of plant material and arrangements are influenced by the environment in which they are placed or by balance with the container used.

With wild plants, it is not incongruent to arrange several together as they would necessarily be from the same season. With cultivated material, much of it imported, it is necessary to give consideration to the season, the size and color of the flowers or else the arrangement will lack coherence and dignity.

As people are becoming extremely fashion-conscious these days, this color sense has become important in ikebana. Many prefer to use flowers of the same color, or combine different shades of the same color. It is good to incorporate the contemporary sense of color in ikebana.

In choosing flowers, it is important to consider the harmony of colors, the sense of volume, the feel of the material, the compatibility with the container and the location for display. It is also necessary for you to arrive at a combination that will bring out the dominent characteristic of each selected material and that they supplement each other.

Points to Remember in Picking Plants

Pick plants either in the early morning or in the evening. Avoid daytime when the plant moisture evaporates in the strong sunshine. When picking them from your garden, be sure to have a bucket of water at hand to put them in immediately after cutting. Once immersed, cut the stems two or three times.

When you transport floral material, wrap it completely in newspapers so it will not be exposed to the wind. After you arrive home, cut again in water and then allow to soak in deep water before arranging.

BASIC METHODS

Basic Forms

The four basic Kozan styles for arranging ikebana follow the natural plant forms.

(1) Upright.......All materials are positioned upright.
(2) Slanted.......Material is arranged slanting to one side.
(3) Spreading....Material is spread sideways or from front to rear.
(4) Cascading...Suspended, material is allowed to flow down.

These basic Kozan styles are applied to both *moribana* and *nageire*. Kozan does not have regulations on the length or angle of the material.

Moribana

The method of arranging ikebana in a shallow container, a basin or a compote, using a *kenzan* or a *shippo* is called *moribana*.

The beginner finds it easier to use the metal needle-point flower holder, *kenzan*. It helps fix the material where desired. The *shippo* holder has open sections where the material is positioned and takes more dexterity.

The fundamental axiom for acquiring a good balance of material is to select three main branches, long, medium and short, and position them to form a scalene triangle.

It is important to fix these branches in a well balanced way. The triangle form is important. Do not have the branches all in one direction, nor on the same plane. With this basic form in place, decorate the base with flowers or plants. Conceal the flower holder. By increasing the number of material from three to five or seven, you can make many variations in arrangements.

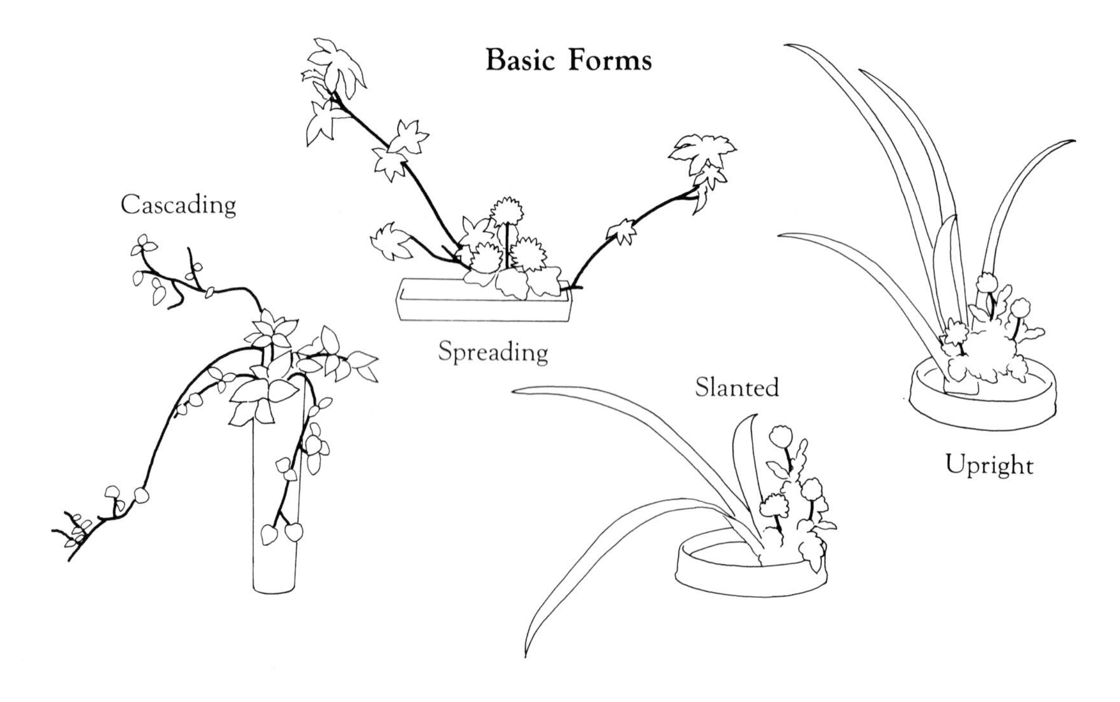

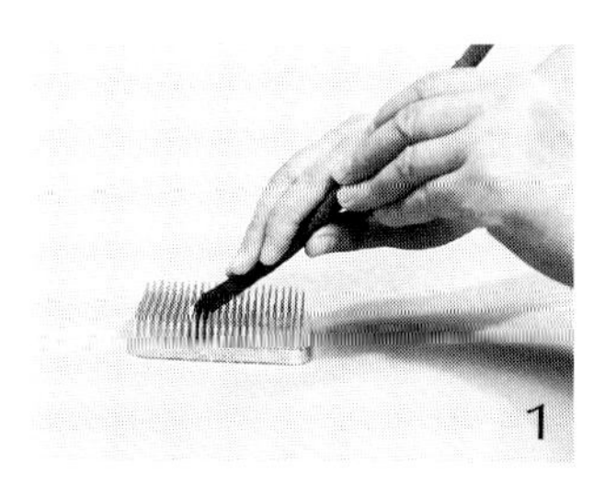

1

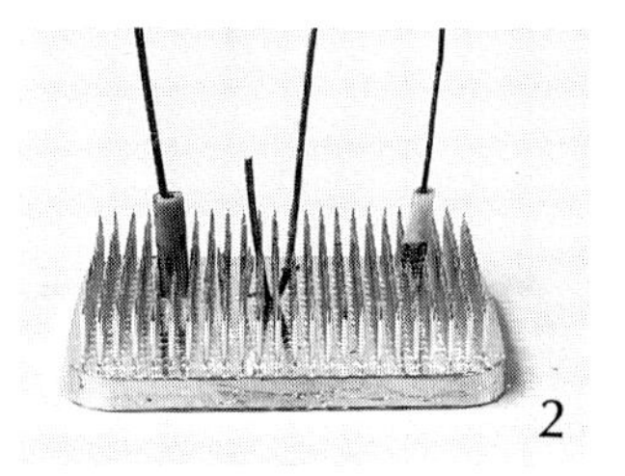

2

3

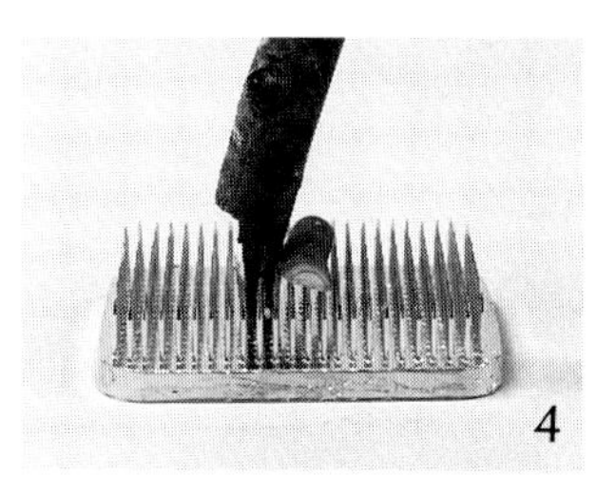

4

5

* The Use of the Kenzan

Kenzan comes in various shapes and sizes. The size and shape of the container and the type of material will determine your choice. Your first purchase should be a large, almost square *kenzan*, 9.5 cm × 7 cm. Other can be added gradually.

Basins also come in many sizes and shapes, but the general rule for using a *kenzan* in a basin is to position it as an oblong facing front. Materials will not so easily fall because it will be better balanced and the arrangement will look firmer.

When considering where the *kenzan* should be placed in the container, avoid the center. A spot about one third from either the right or left side is much more effective in a flat basin. The same ratio can be applied to a rectangular or oval shaped container. A compote, however, is different and the *kenzan* should be placed in the middle.

When placing the *kenzan* in a ceramic or glass container, cut a piece of newspaper the same size as the *kenzan* and put it underneath the *kenzan*. It not only protects the surface of the container, it makes it less slippery. If the container is transparent glass, wrap the *kenzan* with aluminum foil.

* Fixing Material on the Kenzan

When fixing material on the *kenzan*, insert it straight, pushing down until it hits the bottom of the *kenzan*.

- **Branches**—With the slanted cut end facing the rear, press the branch straight down with force until you feel it hit the bottom of the *kenzan*. Tilt it to the desired direction. (Picture 1)
- **Material with Thin Stems**—Some suggested measures include bending the stem end to angle up, wrapping the stem end with something like newspaper, or cutting a short length of a thick stem like chrysanthemum and inserting the thin stem into it. Don't forget to hide the base so these devices cannot be seen from the outside when the arrangement is completed. (Picture 2)
- **Material with Thick, Hollow Stems**—When using material similar to amaryllis with thick, hollow stems, affix a thin twig on the *kenzan* and the put the amaryllis over the twig. (Picture 3)
- **Material with soft stems and heavy heads**—Easter lily and gladiolus are two examples of this kind of material. Support the stem by either a sturdy twig placed sideways or else fixed upright next to it. If you must reposition the material after it has been fixed on the *kenzan*, it is better to cut the end of the stem again as it is porous and it might have been damaged.

A thick branch can also be supported in place by a sturdy length of material placed sideways on the *kenzan* next to the fixed branch. (Picture 4)

- **To Arrange a Long, Heavy Branch or One Bearing Fruit**—Prepare a support, a forked branch or a cross-shape and fix it stably in the *kenzan* as a prop for the branch. The length of the support will be determined by the desired angle for the branch as well as its weight and thickness. (Picture 5)

Nageire

Flowers arranged in a tall vase or pot without the support of a metal holder is called *nageire*.

In the Kozan school the styles for *nageire* are the same as those for *moribana*, upright, slanted, spreading and cascading.

A *nageire* arrangement is free, rather informal as opposed to the stylized *kakubana* which is suitable for the *tokonoma* (alcove). With *nageire*, it is better to aim for a natural, lively arrangement.

The same *moribana* principle of three main branches, long, medium and short, forming a scalene triangle are used in *nageire*, but when a tall vase is used the piece looks better in the cascading or slanted styles.

* Fixing the Branches

You'll have a choice of methods for fixing the material in *nageire* as any of the four styles is suitable. With practice you can master these methods. They will all be useful as the appropriate method will depend largely on the shape of the container and the characteristics of the floral material. It is essential that you learn to make judgement on the right method for a particular container and material.

• **Straight line prop**—Prepare a twig or a dowel the size of the container's diameter and wedge it firmly straight across. (Picture 1)

• **Cross-shape prop**—This prop partitions a wide mouthed container into small sections, making it easier to arrange material. Cut two twigs or dowels the size of the container's diameter and fasten them in the middle with wire to make a cross-shape. (Picture 2)

When a container is wide bodied, but small mouthed, pour water into it about eight-tenths its capacity. Insert a cross-shaped prop about two or three centimeters longer than the diameter of the mouth. (Picture 3) After arranging the material in the container, the prop floats up to the mouth, stabilizing both the prop and materials.

Not all *nageire* is arranged using these props. Sometimes the material itself acts as the stabilizer.

• **Bending**—This method is used with material with elasticity, which does not break easily. Bend the end of the branch upwards and position it against the opposite wall of the container so the tension keeps it in place. This method is suitable for a cylindrical or rectangular container.

• **Cutting**—Determine the length of the material, make a diagonal cut at the stem end the angle that will position the piece where you want it when the angled cut is placed against the inner wall of the container. (Picture 4) This method is not suitable for material with a heavy flower as it would be difficult to keep the balance.

• **Binding**—This works well with thin stemmed material such as baby's breath or statice caspia. Binding several of them together makes them more manageable. (Picture 5)

• **Inserting**—This method is used for fixing thin stemmed material like Chinese miscanthus. Cut a length of hard-stemmed material like chrysanthemum to the measure of the container's diameter and split the stem about one fourth of the length. Wedge the stem into the container, the split side away from the front. Insert the thin-stemmed material into the split. (Picture 6)

Using Scissors

Ikebana scissors are of two types, the *warabi-te* and the *tsuru-te*. The Kozan School uses the *warabi-te*.

To handle the *warabi-te* scissors, the thumb is along one handle of the scissors with the base of the handle resting on the base of thumb. The other four fingers curl around the other handle. A word of caution: do not have your index finger between the handles. It could be hurt in cutting thick material. It's best not to acquire that careless habit from the beginning. (See picture)

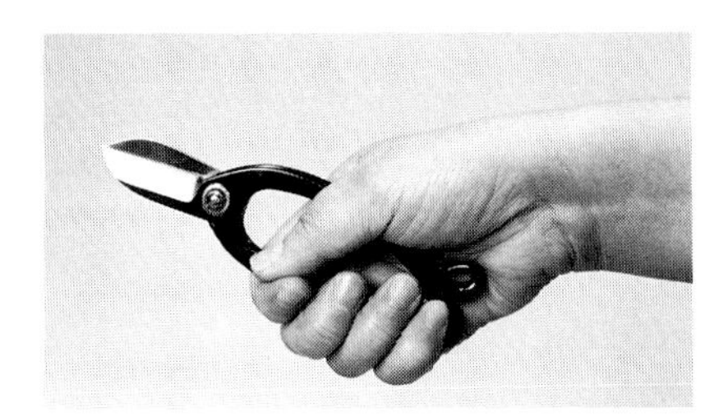

Cutting Stems and Branches

With all material, be sure to cut the stem end once again before arranging it. Remember to handle it with care and cut it quickly.

- **Circular Cut**—For soft plants, thin branches and supple branches, apply the scissors at a right angle to the branch and cut the branch circularly.

When cutting a hollow stem such as that of the amaryllis, the calla lily or the cluster-amaryllis, apply moderate force so not to break the stem and cut slowly while rotating the stem. (Picture 1)

Cut thin stems with the tips of the scissors. Cut thick ones using more of the blade of the scissors.

- **Slanted Cut**—Branches with bark and strong fibers take considerable force to cut, but can be cut quite easily if cut diagonally.

With the scissors at a 45 degree angle to the branch, cut quickly with great force. If the material is very hard and difficult to cut, try several times. If it is to be fixed on a *kenzan*, cut one to two millimeters from the cut end again and make some vertical cuts if it is a thick branch. (Picture 2)

- **Thick Branches**—Use a handsaw. (Picture 3) If a handsaw is not available, nip the branch with the scissors, making cuts around the branch while rotating it. Grasping the branch with both hands., break it.

The cut end of a branch may be split in half for easier cutting.

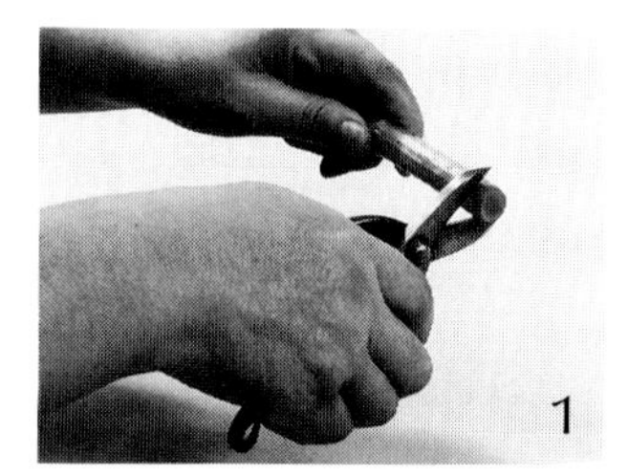
1

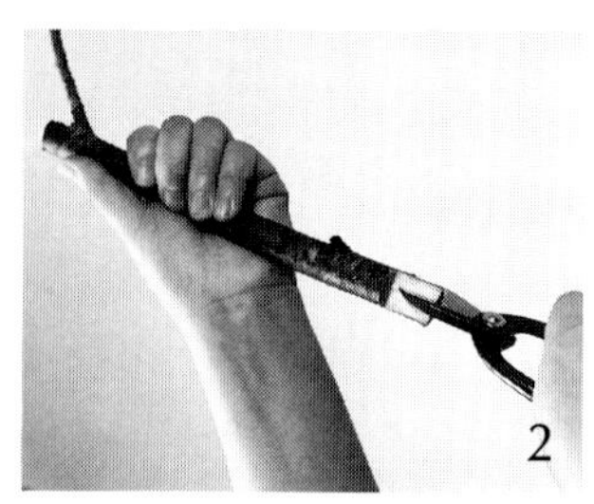
2

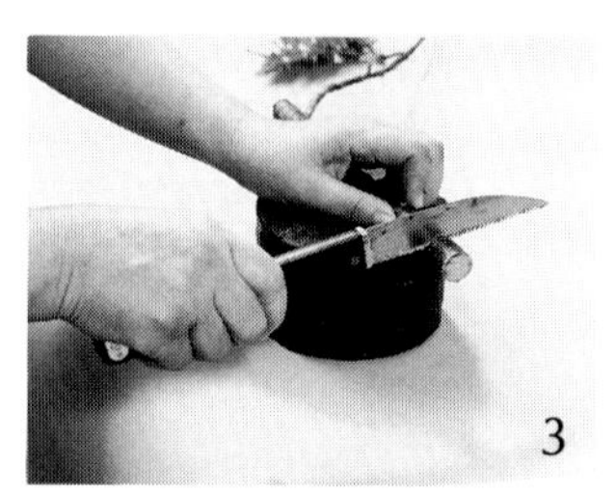
3

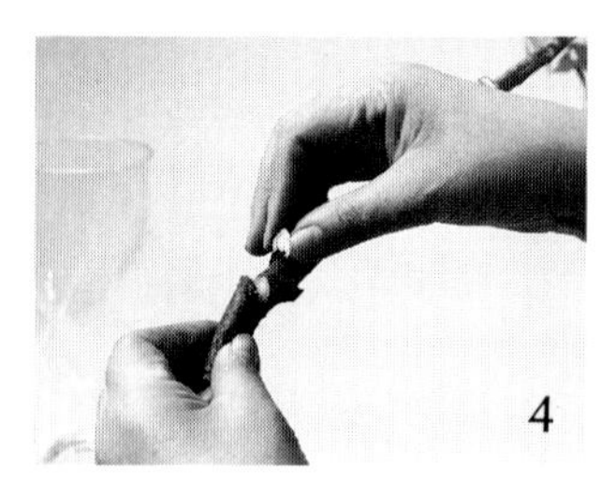
4

Training

Bending a branch to a desired form is called training. This method is used when a branch cannot be arranged easily as in a *nageire* vase, or if you want to modify the shape by bending it slightly.

- **Training by Cutting**—This method is used for thick foliaged trees, hard branches and for material which easily returns to its original shape after training.

For hard, resilient branches like plum or Japanese quince, make a diagonal cut into the branch. With thumbs placed on either side of the cut, press, bending the ends of the branches toward your body, training it with moderate force. To change the direction the branch is facing, make a diagonal cut and carefully twist the branch to the desired direction.

- **Training by Bending**—This method is used for branches and plants which bend easily like willow. Hold both ends of the branch or stem and bend it carefully with moderate force so not to break it. For thin stems, spirea for example, which threaten to break easily, add a twisting motion while training.
- **Training with the Use of a Wedge**—This method is suitable for thick branches and material which breaks very easily. In a branch like that of the lichened pine, make a cut into the branch with a saw, up to two-thirds of the thickness, gently widen the cut with moderate force and insert a wedge into the cut. (Picture 4)

For the wedge, make one in the shape of an isosceles triangle from the same material and soak it in water before inserting it.

- **Training by Crushing**—For flowering plants, train by pressing the stem with the thumb nail, avoiding the joint. You can train it easily if you press the stem lightly with the back of the scissors as if to crush it.

Water Absorption and Preservation

Water absorption preserves the cut branches and flowers, keeping them fresh and making them last longer. Since flowers are living things, it is essential that you cut them in water after purchase. Let them absorb water and then quickly arrange them.

We have investigated many water absorption methods suitable for different species. Our listing here includes the more common, most useful methods.

* **Cut the Stem in Water**—When the cut end of the stem is exposed to the air, it develops a film which prevents the stem from absorbing water. Whether it is a flower purchased at a florist or one collected outdoors, soak it in deep water in a bucket or a bowl and cut the stem once again in the water.

This is the most basic water absorption method proving effective for most flowers and plants. When caring for chrysanthemums, gentians and other such material, the stems must be snapped off by hand under water.

* **Split the Cut End**—With your scissors, make a vertical cut in the cut-end of a thick branch to increase the water absorption area.

* Strip off the bark of the cut end—of all branches, it is most difficult for sprouts to absorb water. It is necessary to not only split the cut-end, but to also strip the bark from the end.

* **Crush the Cut End**—For flowers and plants with hard stems, crush the cut end with a hammer.

* **Soak the Cut End in Hot Water, or Boil the Cut End**—Soaking the cut end of some flowers in hot water opens the suction conduits. This is an effective method for China aster, rose mallow and other such material. To boil the cut ends, put a pinch of salt in the boiling water, wrap the upper part of the material in newspaper to protect the leaves from the steam. Hold the stem in the boiling water for twenty to thirty seconds until the color of the stem end changes color. This method is suitable for material such as peony and *astilbe.*

Material that has soaked in hot water or exposed to boiling water should immediately be dipped in cold water. Arrange them only after they have had time to absorb water.

* **Burn the Cut End**—Burning the cut end will prevent it from rotting. Be sure to first wrap the upper portion of the material in paper soaked with water beforehand to protect it. Burn the cut end with high heat such as a gas flame until it gets red. Immediately soak it in cold water to carbonize it. After soaking the material, cut it to the desired length under water for arranging.

This method is effective for plants that do not absorb water easily such as the rose, marguerite and hydrangea.

* **Lay the Material**—When material looks as though it will wilt, moisten an absorbent piece of paper, newspaper is fine, and lay it in a dark place where it will not be exposed to wind or a draft. This treatment helps bring material back to life.

* **Water the Material While Holding It Upside Down**—Hold the material upside down and sprinkle water over it.

* **Use Chemicals or the Like**—This method helps some material absorb water better.

Alcohol:	maple, wisteria, kerria, wild chrysanthemums and the like.
Vinegar:	pampas grass, oil grass, thistle and the like.
Salt:	Chinese bellflower, willow herb, cosmos, gentian and the like.
Burnt Alum:	Osmund flowering fern, hydrangea and the like.

* **Use a Pump**—For material with spongy stems like the water lily and pond lily which do not absorb water well, use a feeding pump and pump water into the stem from the cut end.

Continued from text pages.

(Page 13)

Material: Cornus (*Cornus officinalis* Sieb. et Zucc.) and pear-bush (*Exochorda racemosa* Rehd.)
Container: Tall vase for nageire

Since the cornus can be shaped, it is possible to reproduce the natural line of a new branch growing out sideways from a major branch by bending it at the base. Pear-bush blossoms were massed at the base of the arrangement to give it stability.

(Page 31, top)

Material: *Koyoraku* azalea (*Menziesia pentandra* Maxim.) and tree peony
Container: Bizen basin

The *koyoraku* azalea bears verticillate leaves at the tips of the branches from which plump yellowish red flowers grow. It looks lovely indeed. This material suits the container.

The combination of a single peony flower with the gentle *koyoraku* azalea gives a dramatic accent.

(Page 31, bottom)

Material: Pear tree and Solomon's seal (*Polygonatum odoratum* Druce)
Container: An ancient Afghanistan receptacle

The way white, five-petalled pear blossoms bloom in corymbous clusters on an old tree branch is nothing less than majestic.

Without inhibitions, I positioned the pear branches in a wide spread from both sides of the dignified, treasured container and arranged large leafed Solomon's seal to create a sense of stability.

(Page 46)

Material: Plantain lily (*Hosta albomarginata* Ohwi.) and white crown campion (*Lychnis gracillima* Makino)
Container: Bamboo basket with handle

The plantain lily grows by the waterside in damp areas. Bearing light purple flowers, it puts forth long stems from heart shaped leaves. I combined it with the white crown campion flowers to create a refreshing impression.

(Page 47, top)

Material: Sunflower
Container: Straw hat

Large flowers give such a strong impression it is essential to give careful consideration to the color combination when arranging them with other material. The sunflower is not easy to arrange by itself as it cannot be shaped. The best solution is to remove most of the leaves and arrange the flowers in a low position.

(Page 47, bottom)

Material: Golden calla lily
Container: Glass compote

The stalks of the yellow flowered calla lily are shorter than those of those with white flowers, but it is still important to let the beauty of those curved stalks stand out. Also make good use of the amusing shape of the leaves, another characteristic of this genus. Be careful not to rearrange the material many times because that would damage the foot of the stalks.

(Page 50)

Material: Lotus
Container: Celadon basin

The lotus thrusts noble flowers from its muddy bed. Since ancient times it has symbolically been a Buddhist flower. This association adds to its sublime beauty, setting it apart from any other flower and makes one feel a bit tense when arranging it.

Tradition has it that the past, present and future should be indicated when arranging lotus. Since lotus does not absorbs water, it is necessary to pump water into the stems.

(Page 51)

Material: *Daimyo* oak, red-berried elder (*Sambucus sieboldii* Bl.) and golden-banded lily
Container: Namako pot

An oak tree bears large, uniquely shaped leaves on rugged branches. Its life force is such that the old leaves will not fall until the new buds come out.

This piece represents manly strength through the characteristics of the oak. The large golden-banded lilies at the base and the red elderberries add a bright touch.

(Page 58)

Material: Bugbane (*Astilbe cimicifuga* L.) and cosmos
Container: Bamboo winnowing basket

Unlike those found at florists, the wild cosmos growing in the fields have slender stems and bear a variety of large and small flowers. By arranging them in a slightly disordered way in a rustic basket and adding bugbane which are beginning to bear small seeds, you can make the material appear truly autumnal.

(Page 59)

Material: *Shinonome* chrysanthemum, *kon-giku* (*Aster ageratoides* Turcz.) and three kinds of small chrysanthemum
Container: Wide mouthed vase

The well liked *shinonome* chrysanthemum is one of the smallest and cutest of all the small chrysanthemum family. The salmon pink color of its flowers resembles the color of clouds at daybreak (*shinonome*). I combined it with *kon-giku* and other small chrysanthemums blooming in my garden.

The flowering time and the height of the buds vary one from the other as they grow in open fields, hills and dales. I had this in mind as I worked on my arrangement.

(Page 74)

Material: Sasanqua (*Camellia sasanqua* Thunb.)
Container: Tall, modern ceramic vase

The *sasanqua*, which grows in Okinawa, Kyushu and southern Shikoku, is a single-petaled flower very similar to the camellia. The sasanqua however, has smaller leaves and the flower petals fall one by one as opposed to the camellia where the whole bloom falls.

The shape of the *sasanqua* branches are without distinctive characteristics, so it is necessary to give much consideration to the container and the material to go with it when arranging. It would also be advisable to pick the flowers before they are in full bloom as the flowers fall easily. For this arrangement, I decided to use only *sasanqua* in an unusual ceramic vase.

(Page 76)

Material: *Su-hsin* wintersweet (*Chimonanthus praecox* L.), Japanese cymbidium (*Cymbidium virescens* Lindl.) and marlberry (*Ardisia japonica* Bl.)
Container: Oval-shaped basin

I arranged the Japanese cymbidium and the marlberry low in the container, as they naturally grow. The thin, long stems and small, red berries of the marlberry and the slender, pliant leaves of the Japanese cymbidium are enough to make a tasteful arrangement, but the addition of the wintersweet gives it dignity.

Japanese cymbidium and marlberry are sold with roots. It is easier to arrange them attached to the roots, so rinse them well in water before arranging. You can plant them in pots or in the ground later.

(Page 85, top)

Material: *Otoko-yōzome* (*Viburnum phlebotrichum Sieb. et Zucc.) and sarumen* calanthe (*Calanthe tricarinate* L.)
Container: Ceramic free-form vase

The *otoko-yōzome*, belonging to the caprifoliaceae family, has pale rose-white, scattered flowerets in the early summer. By autumn they turn into red seed pods.

Calanthe, of the terrestrial showy orchid genus, grows in the high mountains. The Japanese call this type *sarumen*, the mask of the monkey. Its red lebellum suggests the name.

I positioned the container to emphasize the movement of the arrangement and wedged two crossed sticks in its center to support the floral material.

(Page 85, bottom)

Material: Hornbeam (*Carpinus laxiflora* Blume), marsh marigold (*Caltha sibirica* Makino) and white skunk cabbage (*Lysichiton camtschatcense* Schott)
Container: Ancient Afghanistan receptacle

Clean and lovely, the white spathes of the skunk cabbage thrust through the remaining snow in the spring thaw. For this arrangement I added bright yellow marsh marigold flowers, trying to make them look as though they were blooming in the midst of the fresh green leaves. I fixed the flowers, which grow in the damp plains, in a *shippo* and then angled the hornbeam in so it extends vigorously to the left.

(Page 89)

Material: Rose convolvulus (*Calystegia japonica* Choisy) and *teika-kazura* vine (*Trachelospermum asiaticum* Nakai)

Container: Sake bottle

The rose convolvulus, with its lovely pink flowers and the seemingly carefree way the vines grow hither and yon, seem to be smiling at the blazing summer sun. I tried to reproduce the way they twine around the branch of the *teika-kazura* in a *sake* bottle. Remove some of the leaves without impairing the natural shape and the curves of the vine will show. By arranging the vine in the bud stage, you can enjoy the fully bloomed convolvulus the following day without any damage to the petals.

(Page 94)

Material: Bulrush, *hime-zazensō* Japanese skunk cabbage (*Symplocarpu nipponica* Makino), safflower (*Cathamus tinctorius* L.) and white skunk cabbage (*Lysichiton camtschatenses* Schott)

Container: Kirseto basin

The leaves of the *hime-zazensō* bud and grow before the flowers appear. After the leaves wither, the flowers, wrapped in spathes, emerge.

Bulrushes look cool with their long, supple, slender stems. I added the small leaves of the *mizu-basho* which had been growing in the same swamp as the *hime-zazensō* to accentuate this piece.

(Page 104, top)

Material: *Mizo-soba* (*Polygonum thunbergii* Sieb. et Zucc.)

Container: Ceramic vase with three openings

The *mizo-soba* blooms in clusters at the waterside and by the footpaths along the river banks. The colors of the flowers vary from white to a dark pink, probably because of the amount of sunlight they receive and also the difference in the soil.

I positioned all of them in one of the three mouths of this modern vase as though they were peeping out. They absorb water better if a *shippo* is used rather than the *kenzan*.

(Page 104, bottom)

Material: Japanese ampelopsis and *hosoba-no-yamahohko* (*Anaphalis margaritacea* Benth et Hook.)

Container: Compote

Each bunch of *Japanese ampelopsis* grapes has its own individuality, different in shape, a different shade of purple. Each is strikingly beautiful. To make the most of this fascinating attribute, I boldly cut away most of the leaves to give full view of the grapes and show the natural curves of the vines. The feeling of space is enhanced.

LIST OF MATERIALS

English	Latin	Japanese	Pages
Agapanthus	*Agapanthus umbellatus* L'Her.	Agapansasu	34
Akebono camellia	*Camellia japonica* L.	*Akebono-tsubaki*	18
Alpine azalea	*Rhododendron obtusum* Series	*Shakunagé*	25
Amanyu angelica	*Angelica edulis* Miyabe	*Amanyu*	109
Amethyst eryngo	*Eryngium amethystium* L.	*Fringiumu*	56
Arrowwood	*Viburnum furcatum* Blume	*Mushikari*	32
Asparagus	*Asparagus pygmuaeus* Makino	*Tenmondō*	20
Azalea	*Rhododendron* L.	*Tsutsuji*	24
Azalea	*Enkianthus subsesslilis* Makino	*Abura-tsutsuji*	36,120
Baby's breath	*Gypsophila elegans* Bieb.	*Kasumi-sō*	11,17,72
Black lily	*Fritillaria camtschatcensis* ker-Gawl.	*Kuro-yuri*	84
Bluberry	*Vaccinium oldhami* Miq.	*Natsuhaze*	43
Bog billberry	*Vaccinium uliginosum* L.	*Kuromame-no-ki*	115
Bracken	*Pteridium aquilinum* (L.) Huhn	*Warabi*	43,109
Bugbane	*Astilbe cimicifuga* L.	*Sarashina-shōma*	58
Bush clover	*Lespedeza cyrtobotrya* Miq.	*Maruba-hagi*	101
Bush clover	*Lespedeza bicolor* Turcz. var. *japonica* Nakai	*Hagi*	79
Camellia	*Camellia japonica* L.	*Yabu-tsubaki*	15
Cape marigold	*Dimorphotheca sinuata* DC.	*Afurika Kinsenka*	19
Chestnut	*Castanea crenata Sieb.* et Zucc.	*Kuri*	66
Chidakesashi, false goat's beard	*Astilbe microphylla* Knoll	*Chidakesashi*	100
Chilian lily	*Alstroemeria chilensis* Cree.	*Arusutoromeria*	42
China aster	*Gymnaster savatierii* (Makino) Kitamura	*Miyakowasuré*	28
Chinese linden tree	*Tilia miqueliana* Maxim.	*Bodaiju*	70
Chinese miscanthus	*Miscanthus sinensis* Anderss.	*Susuki*	60,69,103,106, 107,119, 120
Chinese monkshood	*Aconitum chilense* Sieb.	*Torikabuto*	56
Cinquefoil	*Potentilla recta*	*Hakuro-bai*	117
Clematis	*Clematis florida* Thunb.	*Tessen*	43
Clethra loosestrife	*Lysimachia clethroides* Duby	*Okatorano-o*	99,103,113
Clintonis	*Clintonia udensis* Trautv. et May.	*Tsubame-omoto*	88
Club-moss	*Lycopodium serratum* Thunb.	*Tōge-shiba*	115
Cockscomb	*Celosia argenteal* L.	*Keitō*	101
Common goldenrod	*Solidago virga-aurea* L. var. *asiatica* Nakai	*Aki-no-kirinsō*	103,112,120
Common spiderwort	*Tradescantia virginiana* L.	*Ōmurasaki-tsuyukusa*	99
Common throat-wort	*Trachelium caeruleum* L.	*Yūgiri-sō*	34
Common yellow loosestrife	*Lysimachia vulgaris* L. var. *davurica* R. Kunth	*Kusaredama*	103,106,116
Cornus	*Cornus officinalis* Sieb. et Zucc.	*Sanshuyu*	13
Cosmos	*Cosmos bipinnatsu* Cav.	*Kosumosu*	58
Cymbidium	*Cymbidium* Sw.	*Sinbijūmu*	72
Daikagura camellia	*Camellia japonica* L.	*Daikagura*	70
Daimyo oak	*Quercus dentata* Thunb.	*Kashiwa*	51
Daiō-matsu, longleaf pine	*Pinus palustris* Mill.	*Daiō-matsu*, Daiō-shō	11

English	Latin	Japanese	Pages
Day lily	*Hemerocallis fulva* L. var. *kwanso* Regel	*Yabu-kanzō*	97
Dandelion	*Taraxacum platycarpum* Dahlst	*Tanpopo*	79
Double-cherry blossom	*Prunus lannesiala* Wilson	*Yae-zakura,*	23,26
Elegant lily	*Lilium elegans* Thunb.	*Sukashi-yuri*	41
Elephant's ear	*Begonia evansiana* Andr.	*Syukaidō*	60
False-spirea	*Sorbus sorbifolia* A.	*Hosaki-nanakamado*	40
Fan columbine	*Aquilegia flavellata* Sieb. et Zucc.	*Odamaki*	83
Flowering crab-apple	*Malus Tschonoskii* (Maxim.) C.K. Schneid.	*Ōzumi*	82
Freesia	*Freesia refracta* Klatt	*Furijya*	20
Fullmoon maple	*Acer japonicum* Thunb.	*Hauchiwa-kaede*	64,119
Fullmoon maple	*Acer shirasawanum* Koidz.	*Ō-itaya-meigetsu*	26,45
Gamazumi viburnum	*Viburnum dilatatum* Thunb.	*Gamazumi*	93,120
Gentian	*Gentiana scabra* Bungei	*Rindō*	65,67,108,118, 120
Gladiolus	*Gladiolus grandavensis* van Houtt.	*Guradiōrasu*	45
Golden calla	*Zantedeschia elliottiana* Engl.	*Ki-kaiu*	47
Golden-banded lily	*Lilium auratum* Lindl.	*Yama-yuri*	51,90,113
Grass-of-Parnassus	*Parnassia palustris* L.	*Umebachi-sō*	115
Great burnet	*Sanguisorba officinalis* L.	*Waremokō*	103,120
Green barley	*Hordeum vulgare* L. var. *hexastichon* Aschers.	*Ōmugi*	92
Greenbrier	*Smilax China* L.	*Sarutori-ibara, Sankirai*	83
Higan-zakura	*Prunus subhirtella* Miq.	*Higan-zakura*	23
Hime-higotai	*Saussurea pulchella* Fisch.	*Hime-higotai*	103
Hime-zazen-sō, Japanese skunk cabbage	*Symplocarpus nipponicus* Makino	*Hime-zazen-sō*	94
Honeysuckle	*Lonicera gracilipes* Mip. var. *glaba* Miq.	*Uguisu-kagura*	95
Hop	*Humulus lupulus* L. var. *cordifolius* Maxim.	*Karahana-sō*	110
Hornbeam	*Carpinus laxiflora* Blume	*Aka-shide*	85
Hosoba-no-yamahōko	*Anaphalis margaritacea* Benth et Hook.	*Hosoba-no-yamahōko*	104
Hydrangea	*Hydrangea macropylla* Seringe	*Ajisai*	39
Iceland poppy	*Papaver nudicaule* L.	*Popi*	21
Ikari-sō barrenwort	*Epimedium grandiflorum* Morr	*Ikari-sō*	82
Indian turnip	*Arisaema sikokianum* Franch. et Sav.	*Yukimochi-sō*	95
Iwa-giku chrysanthemum	*Chrysanthemum nipponicum* Matsumura	*Iwa-giku*	63
Japanese ampelopsis	*Ampelopsis brevipedunculata* Trautv.	*No-budō*	104
Japanese astilbe	*Astilbe odontophylla* Miq.	*Toriashi-shōma*	106
Japanese beautyberry	*Callicarpa dichotoma* Raeus.	*Ko-murasakishikibu*	75
Japanese bellflower	*Platycodon grandiflorum* A. DC.	*Kikyo*	54,62,101,107
Japanese boneset	*Eupatorium japonicum* Thunb.	*Hiyodori-bana*	101,105
Japanese bulrush	*Scirpus lacustris* L.	*Futoi*	37,94
Japanese bulrush	*Scirpus tabernaemontani* Gmel. forma *zebrina* Makino	*Shima-futoi*	48
Japanese cucumber tree	*Magnolia obovata* Thunb.	*Hō-no-ki*	32
Japanese cymbidium	*Cymbidium virescens* Lindley	*Shunran*	76
Japanese hill cherry	*Prunus jamasakura* Sieb., ex Koidz.	*Yama-zakura*	23

English	Latin	Japanese	Pages
Japanese iris	*Iris ensata* Thunb. var. *hortensis* et Nemoto	*Hana-shōbu*	37
Japanese iris	*Iris ensata* Thunb. forma *spontanea* Makino	*No-hanashōbu*	101
Japanese maple	*Acer palmatum* Thunb. var. *amalile* Koidz.	*Iroha-kaede*	23,28
Japanese meadowsweet	*Filipendula purpurea* Maxim.	*Kyo-kanoko*	106
Japanese quince	*Chaenomeles lagenaria* Koidz.	*Boke*	9,12,14
Japanese red pine	*Pinus densiflora* Sieb. et Zucc.	*Me-matsu*	12,71
Japanese spirea	*Spiraea japonica* L. fil	*Shimotsuke*	36,61,88,90
Japanese spirea	*Spiraea betulifolia* Pall	*Maruba-shimotsuke*	112
Japanese stewartia	*Stewartia pseudo-camellia* Maxim.	*Natsutsubaki*	38
Japanese toad-lily	*Tricyrtis hirta* Hook.	*Hototogisu*	66
Japanese udo salad	*Aralia cordata* Thunb.	*Udo*	111
Japanese wake-robin	*Trillium japonicum* Matsum.	*Kinugasa-sō*	82
Japanese white bush clover	*Lespedeza bicolor* Turcz.	*Shirobana-hagi*	64
Japanese winterberry	*Ilex serrata* Thunb.	*Ume-modoki*	73
Japanese witch hazel	*Hamamelis japonica* Sieb. et Zucc.	*Mansaku*	69,117
Kaji-ichigo (Brambles)	*Rubus trifidus* Thunb.	*Kaji-ichigo*	69
Karaito-sō burnet	*Sanguisorba hakusanesis* Makino	*Karaito-sō*	44
Katsura-tree	*Cercidiphyllum japonicum* Sieb. et Zucc.	*Katsura*	105
Kerria	*Kerria japonica* DC.	*Yamabuki*	33
Ko-amacha hydrangea	*Hydrangea macrophylla* Serrata Makino	*Ko-amacha*	54
Kon-giku	*Aster ageratoides* Turcz. var. *ovatsu* Nakai	*Kon-giku*	59
Koyoraku azalea	*Menziesia pentandra* Maxim.	*Koyōraku-tsutsuji*	31
Kudzu-vine	*Pueraria thunbergiana* Benth.	*Kuzu*	107
Kugai-sō	*Veronicastrum sibiricum* Pennell	*Kugai-sō*	98
Kuma-sasa	*Sasa albo-marginata* Makino et Shibata	*Kuma-zasa*	115,118
Kurin-sō	*Primula japonica* A. Gray	*Kurin-sō*	86
Kurumaba-tsukubane-sō, herb-Paris	*Paris verticillata* M. v. Bieb.	*Kurumaba-tsukubanesō*	88
Leucothoe	*Leucothoe grayana* Maxim.	*Hanahiri-no-ki*	71
Lichen covered pine		*Koke-matsu*	9
Lily magnolia	*Magnolia liliflora* Desrouss.	*Mokuren*	16
Lobelia	*Lobelia sessilifolia* Lamb.	*Sawa-gikyo*	108
Lotus	*Nelumbo nucifera* Gaertn.	*Hasu*	50,68
Maple	*Acer palmatum* Thunb.	*Kaede*	32
Marlberry	*Ardisia japonica* Bl	*Yabukōji*	76
Marsh marigold	*Caltha sibirica* Makino forma *erecta* Makino	*Ryukinka*	85
Maule's quince	*Chaenomeles maulei* Schneid.	*Kusaboke*	81
Me-takarakō	*Ligularia stenocephala* Matsumura et Koidz.	*Me-takarakō*	102
Meadow rue	*Thalictrum minus* L. var. *hypoleucum* Miq.	*Aki-karamatsu*	103
Miyako hill cherry	*Prunus jamasakura* Sieb. et Zucc.	*Miyako-yama-zakura*	22
Miyako thistle	*Saussurea Maximowiczii* Herd.	*Miyako-azami*	103
Miyama-hanshozuru clematis	*Clematis alpine* Mill	*Miyama-hanshōzuru*	84
Mizo-soba	*Polygonum thunbergii* Sieb. et Zucc.	*Mizo-soba*	104
Mizu-bashō, white	*Lysichiton camtschatcense* Schott	*Mizu-bashō*	85,94

English	Latin	Japanese	Pages
skunk cabbage			
Mizu-chidori	*Platanthera hologlottis* Maxim.	*Mizu-chidori*	95
Mizu-giku	*Inula ciliaris* Maxim.	*Mizu-giku*	95
Monkshood	*Aconitum japonicum* Thunb.	*Yama-torikabuto*	110
Mountain ash	*Sorbus commixta* Hedlund	*Nanakamado*	32,57
Mountain maple	*Acer palmatum* Thunb. var. *Matsumurae* Makino	*Yama-momiji*	118
Mountain-ash	*Sorbus gracilis* K. Koch	*Nankin-nanakamado*	111
Murasaki-yashio azalea	*Rhododendron albrechtti* Maxim.	*Murasaki-yashio-tsutsuji*	33
Narcissus	*Narcissus tazetta* L.	*Suisen*	12
Nazuna (Shepherd's purse)	*Capsella bursa-pastoris* Medicus	*Nazuna*	79
Nerine japonica	*Lycoris radiata* Herb.	*Higanbana*	109
Nirin-sō	*Anemone flaccida* Fr. Schm.	*Nirin-sō*	95
Nodake	*Pencedanum decursivum* Maxim.	*Nodake*	66
Noriutsugi, panicle hydrangea	*Hydrangea paniculata* Sieb.	*Noriutsugi*	96
Ogi, common reed	*Miscanthus sacchariflorus* Blenth. et Hook L.	*Ogi*	115
Oil grass	*Cymbopogon Spreng.*	*Abura-gaya*	116
Okera	*Atractylis ovata* Thunb. or *Atractylodes japonica* Koidz.	*Okera*	100,106,113
Ōmurasaki azalea	*Rhododendron pulchrum* Sweet	*Ō-murasaki (Tsutsuji)*	29
Oriental Bittersweet	*Celastrus orbiculatus* Thunb.	*Tsuru-umemodoki*	67,110
Osmund	*Osmundastrum cinnamomeum* (L.)	*Yamadori-zenmai*	115
Otogiri-sō	*Hypericum erectum* Thunb. *Angelicaedulis* Miyabe	*Otogiri-sō*	115
Otokoyōzome, rod	*Viburnum phlebotrichum* Sieb. et Zucc.	*Otokoyōzomé*	85,108
Otome lily or rosy lily	*Lilium rubellum* Baker	*Otome-yuri*	35,88
Oyama-bokuchi thistle	*Synurus pungens* Kitam.	*Oyama-bokuchi*	113,116
Pampas grass (Themeda japonica)	*Themeda japonica* Tanaka	*Me-garukaya*	62,100,116
Pansy	*Viola wittrockiana*	*Sumiré*	20
Patrinia	*Patrinia scaboisaefolia* Link	*Ominaeshi*	62,100,101, 103,107,120
Peach blossom	*Prunus persica* Sieb. et Zucc.	*Momo*	17
Pear	*Pyrus serotina* Rehder	*Nashi*	31
Pear-bush	*Exochorda racemosa* (Lindl.) Rehd.	*Rikyubai*	13
Plantain lily	*Hosta albomarginata* Ohwi	*Mizu-gibōshi*	46
Plantain lily	*Hosta undulata* Bailey var. *cromena* F. Maekawa	*Gibōshi*	66
Plume poppy	*Macleya cordata* R. Br.	*Takeni-gusa*	113
Poet's jasmine	*Jasminum officinale* L. var. *grandiflorum* Kobuski	*Sokei*	41
Prairie gentian	*Eustoma russellianum* Griseb.	*Toruko-gikyo*	56

English	Latin	Japanese	Pages
Purple meadow rue	*Thalictrum rochebrunianum* Franch. et Sav.	*Shikin-karamatsu*	56
Rabbit-ear iris	*Iris laevigata* Fischer	*Kakitsubata*	24,68
Rape blossom	*Brassica campestris* L.	*Na-no-hana*	17
Red starlily	*Lilium concolor* Salisb.	*Hime-yuri*	78,119
Red water lily	*Nymphalea tetragona* G.	*Suiren*	37
Red-berried elder	*Sambucus sieboldii* Bl.	*Niwatoko*	51
Red-budded willow	*Salix leucopithecia* Kimura	*Akame-yanagi*	11
Red-veined maple	*Acer rufinerve* Sieb. et Zucc.	*Urihada-kaede*	30,66
Reed	*Phragmites communis* Trinius	*Ashi, Yoshi*	68
Reeves spirea	*Spiraea cantoniensis* Lour.	*Kodemari*	16,21
Rodger's bronze leaf	*Rodegersia podophylla* A. Gray	*Yaguruma-sō*	81
Rose convolvulus	*Calystegia japonica* Coisy	*Hirugao*	89
Rose mallow	*Hibiscus para-mutabilis* L. H. Bailey	*Fuyō*	52
Rose of sharon	*Hibiscus syriacus* L.	*Mukugé*	100
Safflower	*Carthamus tinctorius* L.	*Benibana*	43,94,101
Saga chrysanthemum	*Chrysanthemum morifolium* Ramatuelle	*Saga-giku*	75
Sankaku-i bulrush	*Scirpus triqueter* L.	*Sankaku-i*	97
Sanzun iris		*Sanzun airisu*	90
Sarumen calanthe	*Calanthe tricarinata* Lindl.	*Sarumen-ébiné*	85
Sasanqua	*Camellia sasanqua* Thunb.	*Sazanka*	74
Satsuki	*Rhododendron lateritium* Planch.	*Satsuki*	32
Sawa-hiyodori	*Eupatorium lindleyanum* DC.	*Sawa-hiyodori*	103,107,115
Sawa-oguruma, starwort	*Senecio pierotti*, Miq.	*Sawa-oguruma*	92
Scabious pincushion	*Scabiosa japonica* Mip.	*Matsumushi-sō*	55
Shinonome chrysanthemum	*Chrysanthemum morifolium* Ramatuelle	*Shinonome-giku* ·	59
Shiran	*Bletilla striata Reichb.* fil.	*Shiran*	93
Shirane-aoi mallow	*Glaucidium palmatum* Sieb. et Zucc.	*Shirane-aoi*	90,116
Siberian yarrow	*Achillea sibirica* Ledeb.	*Nokogiri-sō*	91
Siebold campion	*Lychnis sieboldi* v. Houtt	*Matsumoto-sennō*	98,100
Skunk cabbage	*Symplocarpus renifilius* Schott ex Miq.	*Zazen-sō*	79
Snow-on-the-mountain	*Euphorbia marginata* Pursh	*Hatsuyuki-sō*	56
Solomon's seal	*Polygonatum odoratum* (Mill.) Druce	*Amadokoro*	22,28,29,31,36, 43
Solomon's seal	*Polygonatum falcatum* A. Gray	*Naruko-yuri*	90
Showy lily	*Lilium speciosum* Thunb.	*Kanoko-yuri*	53
Spike winter hazel	*Corylopsis spicata* Sieb. et Zucc.	*Tosa-mizuki*	15,45
Spirea thunbergii	*Spiraea thunbergii* Sieb.	*Yukiyanagi*	11,19,35,37
Spray mum		*Supureimamu*	71
St. John's wort	*Hypercium laxum* Thunb.	*Koke-otogiri*	115
St. John's-wort	*Hypericum chinense* L.	*Biyō-yanagi*	44
Star of Bethlehem	*Ornithogalum* L.	*Ō-amana*	45
Star-flowered lily of the valley	*Smilacina japonica* A. Gray	*Yuki-zasa*	117
Statice caspia	*Limonium bellidifolium* Gouan	*Kasupia*	42,45
Stauntonia	*Stauntonia hexaphylla* Decne.	*Mubé*	78
Su-hshin winter sweet	*Chimonanthus praecox* L. var. *concolor* Makino	*Soshin-robai*	76

English	Latin	Japanese	Pages
Sugina (Field horestail)	*Equisetum arvense* L.	*Sugina*	79
Sunflower	*Helianthus annus* L.	*Himawari*	47
Super pink	*Dianthus superbus* L.	*Nadeshiko*	100,101,107
Tamagawa toad-lily	*Tricyrtis latifolia* Maxim.	*Tamagawa-hototogisu*	97,102
Tara vine	*Actinidia arguta* Planch.	*Kuro-zuru*	72
Tebako-momijigasa	*Cacalia tebakoensis* Makino	*Tebako-momijigasa*	87
Teika-kazura	*Trachelospermum asiaticum* Nakai	*Teika-kazura*	89
Tekiri sedge	*Carex kiotensis* Franch. et Sav.	*Tekiri-sugé*	91
Toad lily	*Tricyrtis Japonica* Miq.	*Hototogisu*	108
Toad-lily	*Tricyrtis macropoda* Miq.	*Yama-hototogisu*	108
Tree clethra	*Clethra barbinervis* Sieb. et Zucc.	*Ryobu*	63
Tree peony	*Paeonia suffruticosa* Andrews	*Botan*	31
Tsukubané	*Buckleya Joan* Makino	*Tsukubané*	61
Tsukubane-sō, herb-Paris	*Paris tetraphylla* A. Gray	*Tsukubane-sō*	90,91
Tsukushi, horsetail	*Equisetum arvense* L.	*Tsukushi*	79
Tulip	*Tulipa gesneriana* L.	*Turippu*	11,19
Unryu weeping willow	*Salix matsudana* Koidz.	*Unryu-yanagi*	18,21
Uwamizu cherry	*Prunus grayama* Maxim.	*Uwamizu-zakura*	80
Wake-Robin	*Trillium smallii* Maxim.	*Enrei-sō*	90
Weeping forsythia	*Forsythia suspensa* Vahl	*Rengyo*	16
Wheel lily	*Lilium medeloloides* A. Gray	*Kuruma-yuri*	117
White Japanese spirea	*Spirea japonica* L. fil	*Shirobana-shimotsuke*	106
White burnet	*Sanguisorba albiflora* Makino	*Shirobana-touchisō*	55
White camellia	*Camellia japonica* L.	*Shiratama-tsubaki*	14
White crown campion	*Lychnis gracillima* Makino	*Senjuganpi*	46
White peony	*Paeonia japonica* Miyabe et Takeda	*Yama-shakuyaku*	112
White trumpet lily	*Lilium japonicum* Houtt.	*Teppo-yuri*	49
Wild grapevine	*Vitis coignetiae* Pulliat	*Yama-budō*	114
Willow herb	*Epilobium angustifolium* L.	*Yanagiran*	99
Wisteria	*Wistaria floribunda* (Willd.) DC.	*Fuji*	24
Wormwood	*Artemisia vulgaris.* L. var. *indica* Maxim.	*Yomogi*	115
Wtater hemlock	*Cicuta virosa* L.	*Doku-zeri*	101
Yama-hotarubukuro, bellflower	*Campanula punctata* Lam.	*Yama-hotarubukuro*	87
Yamashiro-giku	*Aster ageratoides* Turcz. var. *adustus* (Maxim.)	*Yama-shirogiku*	108
Yellow pond lily	*Nuphar japonicum* DC.	*Kōhoné*	48
Yellow viotet	*Viola brevistipulate* (Fr. et Sav.) W. Becker	*Ōba-ki-sumiré*	90
Yellow stone crop	*Sedum kamtschaticum* Fisch.	*Kirin-sō*	106
Yoshino cherry	*Prunus yedoensis* Matsumura	*Yoshino-zakura*	23
Yuga-giku	*Aster pinnatifidus* Makino	*Yūga-giku*	64,112
Yulan	*Magnolia denudata* Desrouss.	*Haku-mokuren*	30
Yuzu citron	*Citrus junos* Sieb. ex Tanaka	*Yuzu*	75
Zebra grass	*Miscanthus sinensis* Ander. var. *zebrinus* Matsum.	*Takanoha-susuki*	52

BIBLIOGRAPHY

A Field Guide in Color to Wild Flowers
Encyclopedia of Horticulture. Seibundo-shinkosha, Japan
Encyclopedia of Plants and Flowers. Hamlyn
Japanese Plants. Betti W. Richards and Anne Kaneko. Shufunotomo, Japan
Kansho Shokubutsu-zukan. Bungo Miyazawa. Yokendo, Japan
Makino's New Illustrated Flora of Japan. Tomitaro Makino. Hokuryukan, Japan
Nihon Engei Shokubutsu-zukan. Hoikusha, Japan
The American Heritage Dictionary of the English
The Concise Flowers of Europe. Oleg Polunin. Oxford
The Hamlyn Dictionary of House and Garden. Rob Herwig. Hamlyn
Wild Flowers. John Gilmour. Collins
Wild Flowers of Britain and Northern Europe. Collins